smART

USE YOUR EYES TO BOOST YOUR BRAIN

Adapted from the *New York Times* Bestseller *Visual Intelligence*

AMY E. HERMAN
with HEATHER MACLEAN

SIMON & SCHUSTER BOOKS FOR YOUNG READERS
New York   London   Toronto   Sydney   New Delhi

SIMON & SCHUSTER BOOKS FOR YOUNG READERS

An imprint of Simon & Schuster Children's Publishing Division

1230 Avenue of the Americas, New York, New York 10020

Text © 2016, 2021 by Amy E. Herman

This young reader's edition is adapted from *Visual Intelligence* by Amy E. Herman,
published by Houghton Mifflin Harcourt in 2016

Jacket illustration and design by Laura Eckes © 2022 by Simon & Schuster, Inc.

SIMON & SCHUSTER BOOKS FOR YOUNG READERS
and related marks are trademarks of Simon & Schuster, Inc.

For information about special discounts for bulk purchases, please contact Simon & Schuster
Special Sales at 1-866-506-1949 or business@simonandschuster.com.

The Simon & Schuster Speakers Bureau can bring authors to your live event.
For more information or to book an event, contact the Simon & Schuster Speakers Bureau
at 1-866-248-3049 or visit our website at www.simonspeakers.com.

Interior design by Laura Eckes

The text for this book was set in Adobe Garamond Pro.

Manufactured in China

0622 SCP

First Edition

2 4 6 8 10 9 7 5 3 1

CIP data for this book is available from the Library of Congress.

ISBN 9781665901215

ISBN 9781665901239 (ebook)

To Mrs. Helen Mackenzie,
my sixth grade teacher, who opened my
eyes to the power of words

CONTENTS

How to **SEE** 1

How to **THINK** About What You See   83

How to **TALK** About What You See   125

How to **SEE**

"The world is full of magic
things, patiently waiting for
our senses to grow sharper."

— Author Unknown

Grab something to write with and something to write on so when you see this symbol, you can play along with the activities and games in this book!

CHAPTER 1

YOUR BRAIN IS MAGIC

THE HUMAN BRAIN IS A MYSTERY AND A MARVEL. AND maybe a little bit magical.* It tells our bodies what to do, consciously and unconsciously. It stores our thoughts and memories, regulates our emotions, and, every once in a while, comes up with really great ideas like antibiotics or waffle cones.

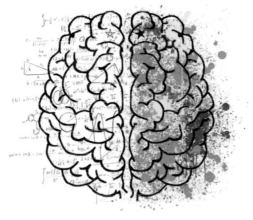

 MAGICAL (adjective): having the power to make impossible things happen; able to create things, including illusions, without the viewer knowing how.

Much like when you practice baseball or the piano, every time you use your brain, you're improving it. For example, look at the earlier drawing.

What do you see?

Pretend you had to describe it to someone who couldn't see it. What would you tell them?

Would you tell them half the drawing was in black-and-white and the other half was in color? Would you mention the sketches and numbers on the left side and the colorful splatters that look like paint on the right?

Does the illustration remind you of anything? If you're thinking "a brain," you're right. It was meant to look like a human brain.

Did any shapes stand out to you?

Did you find the same shape on both sides? If you saw the two stars, good for you! Your brain is tuned in to both details and patterns. If you didn't, go look for them now.

Scientists used to believe that the brain you were born with was the brain you were stuck with and that some people were just born with smarter brains. But as people lived longer, healthier lives and technology advanced, scientists were able to learn more about the human brain. And they discovered some startling things. Such as the brain can heal itself. Or that it can make new pathways and rewire connections. And that it never stops growing. The brain's ability to adapt and change is called "plasticity."*

We can improve our brain's function at any time in our lives, for all of our lives. The more you engage your brain, the quicker, smarter, and more powerful it will be. Which is helpful not just for your future—getting a job or following your passion—but also in the present. A better, faster brain can help you right now. It can help you do better in school,

 "PLASTIC" as a noun refers to the material used to make video game controllers and water bottles. "Plastic" the adjective means "capable of being molded."

have better friendships, be a better judge of situations, and negotiate better deals with the adults in your life (like later bedtimes or a larger allowance). A better, faster brain can help keep you safe, help you solve difficult problems, and help you see what everyone else may have missed.

BRAINY KIDS

In 1905, an eleven-year-old named Frank Epperson was in his San Francisco backyard making his favorite drink—flavored powder stirred into water—when his mother called him inside. He set his cup down and forgot all about it. There was an unseasonal frost overnight, and the next morning Frank found his cup had completely frozen, the stirring stick standing straight up in the colored ice. He tipped the cup upside down, removed it, held the stick, and licked the delicious fruity icicle. He realized other kids might like to do the same, so he intentionally began freezing his flavored water in small cups with sticks and called them "Epsicles." Today the company he started sells two *billion* "Popsicles®" a year.[1]

When Hannah Taylor was five years old, she saw something countless other people had seen before her: a homeless man eating out of a trash can. Instead of just shrugging it off though, Hannah decided to do something about it. Three years later, she founded the Ladybug Foundation to raise awareness and funds for the homeless community. She became a voice for the homeless, speaking to crowds of sixteen thousand people at a time, and so far, she's raised $2 million to help the cause.[2]

HANNAH TAYLOR

When twelve-year-old Jessica Maple's grandmother's house was robbed, she was told by police that since they found no signs of forced entry, the burglar was someone who had used a key to get in. Jessica did her own detective work, though, and discovered a broken window and fingerprints the police had missed in the attached garage. She then thought about what the criminals would do with the stuff they stole and decided they might try to sell it for money. She visited a local pawnshop and found some of her grandmother's belongings there. When she told the police, they were able to interview the shop owner about who had sold them the items, and the suspects were arrested.[3]

JESSICA MAPLE

What did these three kids have in common? They all saw something everyone else had missed.

Want to be the hero in your own life, for your family, or for your community? You don't need superpowers, just a supercharged brain.

Supercharging your brain is easy, and anyone—I mean *anyone*—can do it. It doesn't matter where you go to school or how many books you've read. It doesn't involve memorizing or math. All it takes to increase your brain's capacity for thinking and problem solving, to help you become the next inventor or crime solver or great humanitarian, is three simple steps:

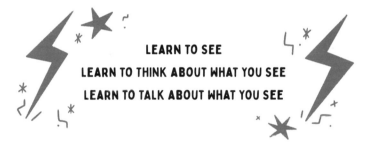

LEARN TO SEE

LEARN TO THINK ABOUT WHAT YOU SEE

LEARN TO TALK ABOUT WHAT YOU SEE

I'm sure you're thinking, as I once did, "But I already know how to see! I've been doing that since I was born!" Followed by, "And anyway, I see with my eyes, not my brain." It turns out that our eyes are actually part of our brain, and the eye and the brain work together in ways we probably never thought about. Let me explain.

You've no doubt learned, from the science teacher and from feeling them with your finger, human eyeballs are round and made up of many parts. There's the pupil—the black circle—and the iris—the colored circle—that work together to control the amount of light let into the eye. Then there's the retina, a thin layer of tissue that covers the back of the eye and converts images into signals for our brain to organize. The retina is a complicated structure more like a computer than a simple pathway to the brain.[4] In fact, it is the brain. (So, technically, when an optometrist looks at your retina during an eye exam, they're looking at your brain!)

When we engage our visual processing system, we're using a full 25 percent of our brain and more than 65 percent of all our brain pathways.[5] So, in reality, we don't "see" with our eyes; we see with our brain.

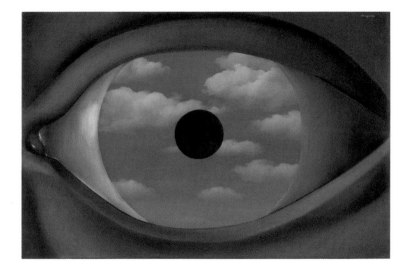

USE IT OR LOSE IT

Our ability to see and make sense of what we see relies on the brain's incredible processing power—a power that depends entirely on the connections in our brains. Scientists have discovered that when we stop flexing our mental "muscles," their speed and accuracy decrease dramatically.[6]

Since our brain controls every function of our body, any slowdown in neural* processing, aka how our brain processes information, will cause a delay in the body's other systems, including how we react to what we see. While slower reflexes and forgetting things are associated with old age, they can also be the result of not exercising our brains enough.

Fortunately, the opposite is also true. Since our brains never stop making new connections, no matter how old we are, we can keep them fast and sharp by continually engaging them. Researchers have found that stimulating our brains in a variety of ways—from studying something new to reading about a concept that makes you think about things in a different way—will increase growth in brain tissue, even for the very oldest humans.[7] If you want to still be able to drive a car, play video games, and remember the lyrics to your favorite song when you're one hundred years old, never stop training your brain.

Want to flex your brain right now? The drawing on page 3 isn't just a representation of the brain with all its "wrinkles"—technically the grooves are called "sulci" and the ridges are "gyri"— it's also a maze! Actually, two mazes. Turn back and see how fast you can move through the LEFT side of the brain maze starting from the opening at the bottom (the brain stem) to the black star outline. Want to feel even smarter? Dare someone older than you to solve the RIGHT side of the maze and see how long it takes them. Come back here when you're done.

"NEURAL" refers to any part of the nervous system, which is made up of the brain, spinal cord, and nerves.

9

Did you notice anything about the right maze? That wasn't a printing error: if you start at the opening on the bottom right, you can't get to the solid black star . . . at least, not if you stay *inside* the lines. Did you read any instructions that said you had to stay inside the lines? I didn't. Who is to say we can't cross the line to get to the star? What if we drew a bridge over one of the lines? Or grabbed a frog to hop us over? Grab a piece of paper to draw three ways you could jump over this solid line:

#1

#2

#3

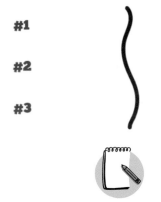

No matter how we exercise our brains, we're making them sharper. Whether you solved the left maze quickly or slowly, your brain still learned from the experience. It will be faster the next time you do a maze and the next time you try to solve any puzzle—on paper or in real life.

Completing the right maze just taught your brain to find alternative, creative answers when you run into an obstacle. This is an extremely useful skill since problems will always be there to get in our way. If we can find a means around them (or over them or through them) we're going to have a lot more success in life.

While there are many different "brain games" you can play to sharpen your wits, I've found the best way to do so is to use something that surrounds us every day: art.

WHY ART?

Art expands the way we see the world and shifts our perspective because everyone's idea of creativity is different. We get to see things, people, and ideas in ways we would have never thought of. Art can transport us to destinations outside our everyday lives and sometimes out of our comfort zones. Art inspires conversation, especially when it makes us squirm. Surprisingly, discomfort and uncertainty bring out the very best in our brains. Harvard psychologists discovered that the brain is most effective at learning new material when our stress hormones are slightly elevated by an unfamiliar experience.[8]

Art gives us that and more. In some paintings, we might see women with noses where their eyes should be, clocks dripping from trees, blue horses, and lots of people screaming. These images are probably very different from the way we see our own world.

Part of the beauty of art, especially the stranger pieces, is that anyone can discuss it, even if you know nothing about art history. In this book, we won't be studying brushstrokes or colors or historical periods. We'll simply be using art as visual data: talking about what we see . . . or what we *think* we see to actually help us see even more. For instance, let's look at this painting:

You don't have to know who painted it, or when it was painted, or why it was painted to describe it. Let's try right now.

What's going on in this painting?

Are the people in the painting indoors or outside?

How many people do you see?

How many different colors are there?

What noise or noises do you hear when you look at this picture?

How would you describe it to someone who couldn't see it?

These are the kinds of questions I'll teach you how to ask yourself as we look at art and then, in how you look at the world around you: questions that will develop your critical thinking skills, teach you how to analyze what you see, and explain it to someone else.

I've been using art to teach people how to see more accurately for eighteen years. I've taught senators, Navy SEALs, and the CEO of Target. The Department of the Army retains me to work with officers before they're deployed to the Middle East. Why? Because when army officers go overseas, they encounter the unexpected and the unknown. Describing what you see in a painting of a figure on a bridge screaming like Kevin McCallister in *Home Alone*—"hands on the side of the face, mouth open, eyes bulging"—uses the same skill set as describing what you see on the first day of school or when you arrive at camp for the very first time. If you can talk about what is happening in a work of art, you can talk about the scenes surrounding your everyday life, anytime, anywhere.

The first thing we're going to do to start the process of supercharging our brains, of training them how to work faster and more accurately, is to slow down.

SLOW DOWN

Alexander Graham Bell was sixty-seven years old when he took the stage at the Friends' School in Washington, DC, to deliver the graduation address to the class of 1914. Sporting a snowy beard that swooped up at the end, the communications pioneer was now a grandfather and nearing the end of his career. Although he was best known for inventing the telephone, he held thirty patents for future contraptions like air-conditioning, metal detectors, and solar panels. So, the crowd was surprised when he confessed that he didn't always take the time to really look around him.

He'd recently taken a walk at his family's property in Nova Scotia, a place he thought he knew everything about. He was shocked to discover a moss-covered valley that led to the sea.

"We are all too much inclined," he said, "to walk through life with our eyes shut. There are things all 'round us and right at our very feet that we have never seen, because we have never really looked."[9]

We live in an incredibly fast-paced world that demands our attention 24/7. And while our brains have unlimited potential, our attention is finite. We'll only see what we really look for, and if we look too fast, we can miss a lot. What other amazing innovations did Bell miss by not always paying attention? What have we missed?

Do you remember the first painting in this book? Not the painting we just saw of the figure screaming on a bridge, but the square painting made up of different shapes right before Chapter 1 began? Without turning back, draw as much of the painting as you can remember.

If you're like most people, you saw it but didn't study it. You might have flipped right past it because there were no instructions to stop and stare at it. Don't wait for someone to tell you to use your brain to gather as much information as you can wherever you are. You just might discover what you need to change the world!

Slowing down doesn't mean moving at a slow pace. It just means taking a few extra minutes to absorb what you are seeing. Details, patterns, and relationships take time to recognize. Information can be missed if we rush past it.

Let's go back to the screaming painting on page 12. Only this time, really examine it. Set a timer for two minutes. On a separate piece of paper, write down as many details as you can about the painting. Just a list. No sentences. Come back here when you're done.

Did you write down that the person screaming has no hair?

Did you note the number of people in the painting?

Did you see the boats in the background? How many? If not, go back and count them now.

How many rails are on the bridge?

Did you see the border on the right side of the painting?

How much more did you notice in the painting—called *The Scream* by Edvard Munch—when you looked at it longer and harder?

(Answers: There are three people, two boats, and three railings in the painting.)

Let's flex our brain muscles again with another painting. Set a timer for one minute. Now turn back to that very first painting on page 1. When you're done studying it, come back here.

Now draw as much of the painting as you can remember.

How much more did you see this time? How much more accurate is this picture than your first one?

We're going to look at the painting one more time, but instead of drawing it, I'm going to ask you questions about it, so tune your eyes and your brain in to catching as many elements—both big and small—as you can. Set a timer for two minutes, then come back here when you're done.

The painting you were just looking at has one of the longest titles ever: *Fifty Abstract Paintings Which as Seen from Two Yards Change into Three Lenins Masquerading as Chinese and as Seen from Six Yards Appear as the Head of a Royal Bengal Tiger.* It was painted in 1963 by Salvador Dalí. Let's find out how much you saw:

1. What shapes did you see?
2. Did you see any human faces? If so, how many?
3. Did you see an animal's face? If so, what kind?

4. Did you see eyes? How many? What color?

5. Did you see tears (as in crying)?

6. Did you see teeth?

7. Did you see that some teeth were sharp and some were dull?

8. Did you see whiskers?

9. Did you see stitches?

10. Did you see a bicycle?

Here are the answers:

1. There are many shapes in the painting, including squares, circles, triangles, diamonds, ovals, cones, cylinders, and an assortment of polygons. Bonus points if you listed any of the types of triangles: right, equilateral, obtuse, or scalene. There were no rectangles.

2. There are three human faces.

3. There is a tiger's face.

4. There are eight eyes: three human and one animal. Only the animal's eyes are fully opened. They are a yellow/amber/brown color.

5. The person on the upper right has what appear to be tears, or some other liquid, coming from their eye.

6. The tiger is showing its top and bottom teeth. There are fourteen teeth in total: eight on top and six on the bottom. Four are large fangs.

7. Ten of the tiger's teeth are sharp, while four are not. Good for you if you noticed the difference!

8. There are what appear to be whiskers on the tiger's face, two sets of which also form mustaches on the human faces.

9. Two of the humans' eyes are stitched shut. There are five stitches in total.

10. Trick question! There was no bicycle.

KEEP TRAINING YOUR BRAIN

As we've just seen, the longer and more attentively we look at something, the more we will find. Many of the world's greatest thinkers, like Leonardo da Vinci and Steve Jobs, believed that invention was more about recognizing the potential in things than simply creating new stuff. We can uncover exciting possibilities by just opening our eyes, turning on our brains, tuning in, and paying attention. Sir Isaac Newton agreed, saying, "If I have ever made any valuable discoveries, it has been owing more to patient attention than to any other talent."[10] We *all* have the ability to observe in different ways and make discoveries that will lead to great things. We just need to be prepared to notice them.

Let's practice some more. This is *Past Times* by the artist Kerry James Marshall. Mentally check off the following items as you spot them:

- [x] A dog
- [x] Seven birds
- [x] A blue croquet ball
- [x] Clouds
- [x] The word "heart"
- [x] The word "heart" again
- [x] A water-skier
- [x] The sun
- [x] Sunglasses
- [x] A park bench

Great! Let's try another. Grab a new sheet of paper if you need one.

Here are two pieces of art next to each other.

What are three differences between the images? What are three things they have in common?

Now show the two images to someone else. Ask them to come up with three differences and three similarities and write down what they tell you.

Compare your lists. Was anything the same? Why do you think your lists might have been different?

Let's do one more. In honor of our friend Frank Epperson, inventor of the Popsicle®, and the other incredibly brainy kids who have helped make our world a little sweeter, let's take a look at this work of art:

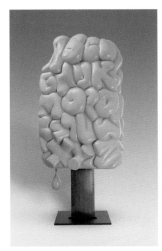

What does it look like?

What else does it remind you of?

Do you see a Popsicle?

Do you see any letters of the alphabet? If so, which letters?

Do you see anything else?

I bet you can already feel your brain getting faster and sharper! The more you practice actively looking, the more you'll uncover.

Did you immediately see a Popsicle? Did you remember that Frank Epperson was its inventor and helped make the world a little "sweeter"?

While observing the sculpture, did you think it looked like a brain? If so, it might be because I purposefully used the word "brainy" right before it.

When I first glanced at the sculpture, I thought of squishy intestines.

Gross, right? Maybe it's because of the color, but it's more likely because I had just worked with a group of nurses, and we had talked a lot about anatomy.

The human brain is amazing. As I mentioned, it can heal itself, learn new things, and get smarter every day of our lives. But it's not perfect. We don't have unlimited attention spans or flawless memories. Sometimes our brains can even be unintentionally tricked by limited sleep or stress, or intentionally by a carefully planted word or recent experience.

You've already seen how much more powerful your brain can be when you engage it. Now, to unleash our brain's full potential, we're going to learn how to overcome some of its weaknesses—like biases and blind spots.

CHAPTER 2

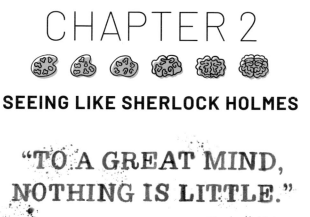

SEEING LIKE SHERLOCK HOLMES

"TO A GREAT MIND, NOTHING IS LITTLE."

—Sherlock Holmes

WHAT DO A STUDENT, AN EYE DOCTOR, AND ONE OF THE world's best-selling authors have in common? A lot, actually, since they are all the same person: Sir Arthur Conan Doyle, creator of the famous detective Sherlock Holmes.

When Doyle first opened his medical practice in 1882, he didn't have many patients, so he wrote stories to bring in extra money.[11] Doyle turned to one of his favorite medical school professors for inspiration—Dr. Joseph Bell, a tall, eccentric man who often wore a cloak and tweed hunting cap and could tell things about people just by looking at them.[12]

During one of Dr. Bell's classes, a man came in to be diagnosed by his students. Due to his clear limp, the students guessed the man had hip problems, but Dr. Bell shook his head and pointed out the slits the man had cut in his shoes to ease his foot pain.[13] The students had

just noticed the most obvious and missed that detail completely.

Dr. Bell could identify people who smoked by looking at their lips, what job a person had by noticing the calluses on their thumbs, and whether someone worked inside or outside by the color of their tan.[14] He was often called in by the British police to work on hard-to-solve cases, including the incidents involving the famous Jack the Ripper.

Dr. Bell believed that nothing was more important to discovery—in medicine, criminal law, or life in general—than finely tuned observation skills. He let no detail, however small, escape his notice, frequently pointing out tattoos, accents, skin markings, scars, and clothing down to the color of the soil on someone's shoes that others failed to see.

"Glance at a man," Dr. Bell instructed, "and you find his means of livelihood on his hands and the rest of his story in his gait, mannerisms, watch-chain ornaments, and the lint adhering to his clothes."[15]

He was fond of chanting in class, "Use your eyes! Use your eyes!"[16]

Dr. Bell was quick to note the difference, though, between passively seeing something and actively assessing it. He concluded, "Most people see but do not observe."[17]

What's the difference? Sir Arthur Conan Doyle had Sherlock Holmes explain the distinctions between seeing and observing in one of his first stories.[18] When his assistant, Dr. Watson, claims to have eyes just as good as Holmes, the detective asks Watson if he saw the stairs they just climbed. Watson responds, "Hundreds of times."

Holmes asks, "Then how many are there?"

"How many? I don't know," Watson replies.

"Quite so! You have not observed. And yet you have seen . . . Now, I know that there are seventeen steps, because I have both seen and observed."

Seeing is just looking at something, but observing is so much more. Observing means noticing the details—large and small—about what you see.

Let's take the same test:

Picture a set of stairs you have climbed hundreds of times, maybe leading up to the front door to your house or your school. Can you see them? Good. Grab a piece of paper and draw your house or the building and the steps.

Now, how many steps are there? Are you positive?

We may see the steps, but most of us don't note how many there are. We see, but we do not observe.

It's not entirely our fault; our brain can handle only so much information. And we're constantly giving our brains a lot to process. But when we take the time to really observe, it is amazing how much more information we will have about the thing that we are looking at.

Look at the following picture for just fifteen seconds. (Set a timer!)

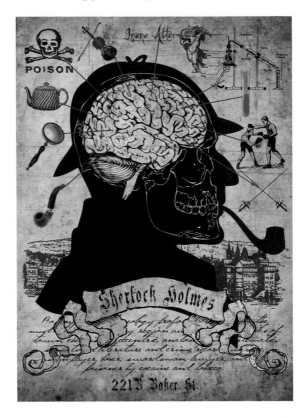

Now cover it and write down everything you can remember about the picture.

How many things did you remember?

By our count, there are at least twenty-five different objects in the picture.

Without looking, list all the things there were at least two of.

Did you see:

- ☑ 2 pipes
- ☑ 2 people
- ☒ 2 swords
- ☑ 2 boxing gloves
- ☑ 2 test tubes
- ☒ 2 buildings
- ☑ 2 doors
- ☑ 2 windows
- ☑ 2 trees
- ☑ 2 curls in the banner
- ☑ 2 skulls
- ☑ 2 bones
- ☒ 2 teeth
- ☑ 2 words
- ☑ 2 numbers
- ☒ 2 names
- ☑ Bonus points if you can remember the two names!

(Bonus points answer: Sherlock Holmes and Irene Adler.)

We could go even further and count more specific things, like the number of capital *B*s. We could also count more general things, like how many items require fire to get started. Even though our eyes saw everything, our brain didn't register all of it. It couldn't. Like computers and video game consoles, our brain doesn't have an unlimited capacity to process data. It has to select what to pay attention to and what to ignore.

And what our brain ignores can be surprising, especially if we're concentrating on something else. At times we miss something that is right in front of us, and then we ask, "How did I not see that?" The answer is that when you are focused on one thing, it is so easy to miss others that are happening at the same time. This might be good when a single task requires all our attention, but we need to be aware that there are things we are missing. It is good to know what we don't know.

MONKEY BUSINESS

Have you ever been searching for something, like your favorite jacket, and finally found it someplace you'd already looked? It's not you; it's your brain! It's an actual phenomenon, and it happens to everyone: parents and presidents, dog walkers and doctors.

Let me give you an example. Radiologists* are doctors who look for an injury or illness by analyzing X-rays and other images inside the human body.[19] They are great at seeing signs of sickness that might just look like a shadow to someone else. Researchers at Harvard Medical School sent the following slide of human lungs to a group of radiologists and told them to look for any abnormal growths:

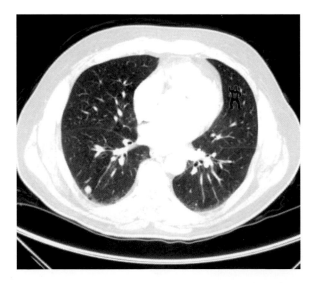

The radiologists looked, but *83 percent* of them didn't mention the gorilla dancing in the upper-right corner.[20] Did you see it?

Sometimes when we're concentrating on one thing, we miss everything else, even something as big as King Kong!

WHAT DO YOU SEE?

For more than ten years I've shown the next photograph to the adults I teach, and I always ask the same simple question: What do you see? I'll ask you the same. In just one sentence, tell me what you see.

People tell me there's a person walking by a large tree and a bench. Some of them mention the fence. Some notice that the bushes are missing leaves. Some say the person is looking down or holding something. But about half the people who view this photograph *don't mention the giant letter* C *in the background.*

"RADIOLOGY" is the science of wireless energy waves that can be used to create pictures of things that are hard to see, like bones inside the body. "Radio-" refers to radiation, a type of light wave used in X-rays, although radiologists also use other types of energy, like sound waves.

Although it uses a small amount of radiation, an X-ray will not give you, or your friendly neighborhood spider, radioactive powers.

Did you see it? Show the photograph to someone else without telling them anything more than "tell me what you see in one sentence" and see if they notice it.

Is it important to notice the C? It is if you're trying to figure out where or when this photograph was taken.

The sixty-foot-high C is painted on a rock wall across from Columbia University in New York City. It first appeared in all white in 1955 and was repainted blue and white in 1986.[21] Since it takes up most of the photograph, it's a good test of your observation skills.

There's nothing wrong with anyone who didn't see the C. Most people just haven't sharpened their observation skills because they haven't seen the need. Missing a dancing ape or a giant capital letter might not seem important right now while you're reading a book, but what about when you're babysitting, riding a bike, or just crossing the street? The thing we don't notice could get us in trouble or stop us from doing what needs to get done. Of all the hundreds of students who sat in Dr. Bell's classes, only one—Sir Arthur Conan Doyle—was smart enough to turn what he saw and heard into a character who starred in fifty-six stories, forty-eight movies, and tons of comic books, cartoons, and television shows.

So how can we learn to improve the way we see? The same way we make progress in any other area: with practice.

Samuel Renshaw, an American psychologist whose research on vision helped the armed forces quickly recognize enemy aircraft during World War II, believed that "proper seeing is a skill which needs to be learned, like playing the piano, speaking French, or playing good golf."[22] He claimed that just like a pianist's fingers, the eyes could be trained to perform better. Multiple studies have confirmed that we can dramatically increase our brain's capacity for memory and attention to detail by training it.[23] How? With challenging visual attention tasks . . . like looking at art.

OBSERVING ART

For the past twenty years, professors at Yale University have helped medical students upgrade their observation abilities by looking at art. Let's pretend to be doctors for a moment, like Arthur Conan Doyle, and study art like Sherlock Holmes.

Let's examine the following painting:

We'll start with the basics.

How many people are in this painting? Who appears to be the patient?

The patient appears to be a young girl sitting in a chair with her feet up, a pillow behind her head, and a red blanket across her legs.

Do we know what's wrong with the girl?

No, but we can figure out quite a lot from studying the scene.

Do you think the girl has a broken leg? Why or why not?

The girl's legs are covered in a blanket, and she is not touching them or showing them to anyone, so she probably doesn't have a broken leg. We can't say for sure though, because we can't see her legs.

She is smiling and holding her arm out for the boy who seems to be checking her pulse. She could have a stomachache, or her throat might hurt, or both.

Do you think the girl is seriously ill? Why or why not?

The doctors I know who have studied art to be more accurate observers have told me that they used to focus only on the patient and the bed, but now they assess everything in a room. For instance, the other children in the room tell us many things. They are involved in their own activities and do not seem terribly upset or worried about the girl in the chair. If the little girl were very sick, the people around her would most likely look worried.

What other things can we learn about the girl from the rest of the scene?

We can see that she is in a room with a rug, toys, and a lot of furniture. Her face, dress, socks and shoes appear to be clean and she is smiling. There are shadows on the wall, which means there is some sort of light in the room, and we can actually see the reflection of the window in the mirror above the fireplace. In the right corner, we see two women walking slowly towards the room with the children. These all suggest that the girl seems well cared for and not in any true danger of being seriously sick. Knowing this helps us figure out how to best help her. If she were alone on the street with dirty clothes, she might need help in other areas of her life.

Let's look at our next patient:

Again, we'll start with the basics. *How many people are in this painting? Who is the patient?*

The patient appears to be a young woman with black hair in a colorful wrap or pajamas. She has a red dot on her forehead. In India this is called a bindi, so she might be from that part of the world or wear it as part of her religion.

What can we see the girl doing?

She is alone lying on a bed propped up on her left elbow with her left hand resting against her face. There is an open letter in her right hand. She is looking up and has what appears to be a slight frown on her face. She doesn't seem to have any physical injuries that we can see. Does that mean she is uninjured? No. She could have internal or mental pain. Her expression suggests she is not well.

What can we learn about her from the rest of the scene?

She is on an ornate, carved bed draped with sheer curtains. She is covered with a red blanket and leaning against a round, dark blue pillow.

She's wearing three strands of pearls and another necklace, two rings that we can see, and two bracelets. Her hair is neat, and her face is clean. These all suggest that the girl is well cared for.

Looking at the clues in the painting, what do you think might be wrong with her?

The opened letter in her hand offers the best guess. She has received news that has left her heartsick. The work, by famous Indian painter Raja Ravi Varma, is titled *Disappointed*.

One of my students started viewing art to increase her observation skills when she was still in medical school.[24] She found the practice helped her notice more in her everyday life and at her job.

"I had no idea how much I was missing," she remembers. "I like to think of myself as a very observant person, and I didn't see the Columbia University C staring me right in the face! I felt like I had been walking around with smudged glasses coloring everything, and I didn't even know I was wearing them!"

After learning how to observe rather than just see, she noticed the way she looked at her patients changed dramatically.

"Where I used to just see flowers in a room as a sign of an ill patient, I now pay attention to what kind they are and if they're wilting, who sent them and when," she tells me.

She now also notes what stuffed animals may be lying on the windowsill, what TV show the patient is watching, and what books are on the bedside table.

"These new details that I'd never noticed before might not tell me a diagnosis," she explains, "but they give me something just as important: information about what motivates the patient."

For instance, if a doctor knows that a patient likes to build model trains, they can talk about how soon the patient can return to that activity, which can speed up a patient's recovery.

Like any other skill, observation can be mastered with practice. At first you have to do this on purpose, but after some time, it will become automatic. Neuroscientists believe that practicing new skills rearranges the brain's internal connections. This means we can wire our brains to see even more.

We can do this with exercises that improve our attention and memory . . . by looking at more art!

MORE, PLEASE

Let's practice with another painting. Set a timer and study the following work of art for one full minute:

Now cover the painting and let's see what you saw.

How many objects were on the table?

What were they?

Describe the painting with as much detail as you can remember.

If you can recall there were five items on the table—a glass, a bottle, a knife, a fork, and a plate with a slice of something on it with an eye in the middle of it—then good for you! If you went on to write that the glass was empty, the bottle full, they were above the plate and utensils, that the fork was to the right of the plate, and the green-handled knife to the right of the fork, and the eye was blue-gray, even better!

What food was on the plate? I've heard "a pancake" quite often, but if you look closely you can see thin white bits of fat. It's really a piece of ham. Bonus points if you noticed the dark red staining on the glass. Another bonus if you noticed that the fork is facedown on the table.

Now let's *really* observe. Go back and look at the painting again but even more closely, more slowly this time.

Look carefully at the stain on the side of the glass. Why is it there if the bottle is full?

Notice the light reflecting off the surface of the bottle, glass, and silverware. Which direction are the shadows pointing? What could be causing the reflection and shadows?

Think about whether everything is really on a table. Could it be somewhere else? Maybe glued to a wall?

Uncovering more questions and more details the longer we look is how we know we're not just seeing but observing.

Now, without turning back, draw the painting yourself, capturing as many details as you can.

Compare it with the original. Did you miss anything? Add those details to your drawing.

To further enhance your memory, wait an hour and then draw the painting again. After you do this a second time, go back and correct it with any missing information.

You can also practice on a single everyday object: your watch, your backpack, or a water bottle. Select something with a lot of detail and really study it for one full minute. Then put it away or cover it up and write down as many details—shapes, colors, textures, words, measurements—as you can. Retrieve the object but instead of subtracting time, add more of it. Observe the same object for three times as long, or three minutes, and see how much more you can find. Do this with a different item every day for a week, and you will notice by the end how the practice has increased your ability to focus and remember what you've seen.

The more you exercise your memory skills, the more you will remember.

The more you consciously observe your environment, the more natural the process will become.

To engage your sense of awareness, go outside at lunchtime, plant yourself in one spot, and practice observing every single thing that crosses your path. Doing so will help train your eyes to look beyond what's right in front of you or what you are used to seeing.

One final test: Do you remember the illustration at the beginning of this chapter on page 24? Can you picture it? I'll give you a hint: it shows Sherlock Holmes looking at a tree.

If you can't remember it, that's okay. Many of us have learned to skim or skip over the beginnings of things, but when we do that, we're possibly missing really important information. We're going to learn, starting right now, how not to do that.

Turn back to the illustration on page 24 to answer the following questions:

How many people are in the image?

How many feet are there?

How many hands?

How many fingers?

There are two people in the illustration, Sherlock Holmes and Dr. Watson. Holmes, with the pipe and magnifying glass, is on top of a rock on top of a hill, looking at what appears to be a hand hanging from a dead tree. Watson, holding a walking stick as tall as he is, stands lower than Holmes and to his left.

How many feet are there? We only see two, but we can guess that Watson has two feet we cannot see.

How many hands are there? We only see four, although unless Holmes or Watson are missing a hand, there are six in total. One hand hangs from the tree, another reaches out from the rock. (Did you see that one? If not, go back and look for it.)

How many fingers? We can see nineteen. If Holmes and Watson each have both hands, then the total count of fingers is twenty-nine.

Extra credit: Did you notice the rock Holmes is standing on looks like a skull?

Neither Dr. Joseph Bell nor doctor/author Arthur Conan Doyle had superpowers. They weren't able to see more because they were born with extra skills. They practiced using their powers of observation on a daily basis. We all have the same abilities; we just don't always use them. If we choose to take the extra step and really observe when we're looking around us, imagine what we might discover!

While we are all capable of increasing our observation skills, to truly harness them and see the way Sherlock Holmes did, we also need to understand the various filters that impair our vision.

CHAPTER 3

FACTS VERSUS FILTERS

WE CAN TRAIN OUR BRAINS TO SEE MORE AND SEE BET-
ter, but that doesn't mean we all see things the same way. To prove this,
Samuel Renshaw, a vision researcher who worked with the armed forces
during World War II, would show people the following photograph:

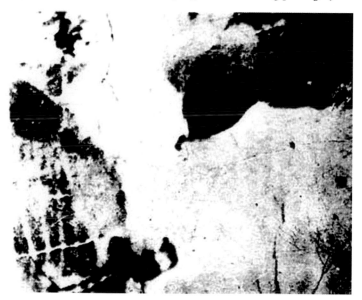

What do you see?

The first time I saw it, I was convinced it wasn't even a photograph, maybe just an inkblot. It is an actual black-and-white photograph from the early twentieth century, but I couldn't see anything but black splotches.

Then I got a hint: it's a four-legged mammal. Do you see an animal? If so, which one?

I saw a cat, a bat, or maybe a platypus. None of those is correct.

It's a cow. Do you see it now?

Don't worry if you can't. I didn't, and more than half the people I've shown it to don't see it either. Perform your own experiment on people around you and count how many see the cow, and if they don't, what do they see?

You probably got some wild guesses, as I did. People have told me they see a blimp, a dragon, and a woman shopping for bras! Even when I tell them it's a cow, most people can't see it until I outline it for them:

Let's try it again with another image.

What do you see?

Take a poll of the people around you.

Is it a green tree with a split trunk against a white background or is it the profile of two faces facng each other? Is either answer correct or both?

Go back to the first photograph and see if you can see faces now. If you still can't, try covering the top part of the tree with your hand.

It seems obvious that we all see things differently. Yet we constantly forget and act as if there was only one, true way to see.

We should not assume that:

* Anyone else sees what *we* see
* We see what *they* see
* Either of us accurately sees *what's really there.*

The way our brains choose to sort through the millions of bits of information available is unique to us and our own perceptual filters.

 PERCEPTUAL FILTERS (noun): the elements of your unique life experiences that color the way you take in and process new information.

PERCEPTUAL FILTERS

No two people will see anything exactly the same way. The biology you inherited from your parents and the preferences you learned growing up will influence the way you see the world. We all observe, notice, and gather information differently, but we also perceive what we've gathered differently.

Perception is how we interpret the information we observe. Think of it as an internal filter. Perception can color, cloud, or change what really exists into what we think we are seeing.[25]

Much like seeing, the process of perceiving is subtle, automatic, and hard to recognize if we're not consciously aware of it. Want to feel it right now?

1. Look back at the photographs on pages 41 and 43.
2. Try *not* to see the cow and the faces.

It's impossible. No matter what crazy thing your mind was creating before, once you see the cow and the faces, you can't see anything else. Why? The power of your new knowledge—that it is a cow and two faces—has effectively erased your previous perceptions.

This happens every time we see, don't see, and can't unsee something. Being aware of how easily our perceptions can change, and refuse to unchange, will help us pay attention to them.

To be able to see something more accurately, we shouldn't rely on the idea that someone else sees or interprets things the way we do. If we stop investigating what we think we see, we could be missing a lot of information. If after viewing the first black-and-white image, I concluded that I saw a platypus and put it away, I might never have learned that the photograph really showed a cow. And if I relayed my experience to others as fact—"this is a photo of a platypus"—I would be spreading incorrect information.

To garner the most accurate picture of anything, we also need to recognize others' perceptions and points of view. How do we find out what other people see or think they see? We don't have to look any further than to the art that is outside of a museum and people's reaction to it.

When *The Collective* by Paul Bobrowitz was created and shown in Appleton, Wisconsin, in 2019, the reviews were very good and very bad. Some said the sculpture, made from used propane tanks, was "ugly, creepy, disgusting, and horrifying." Others called it "delightful, interesting, and thought-provoking." One resident said it was "scary" and that the little kids in the neighborhood were "terrified" of it.[26]

Show this image to the people around you and note how many of them use any of the words below to describe the sculpture:

Ugly   Delightful   Scary   Thought-Provoking

Of course, not everyone is going to like the same things, but think about *why* the people you asked answered the way they did. Did their age or job or hobbies affect their answers? A forty-year-old will probably see it differently than a three-year-old. Someone who adores modern art will see it differently than someone who hates modern art. Someone who works for a propane company will see it differently than someone who doesn't.

Do you think your answers might change if the sculpture were in front of your house?

Perception is also shaped by a person's values, upbringing, and culture. Did the males you asked see it differently than the females? Do you think someone in India or Russia would see it differently than someone in Hawaii or Kansas? Since our world is made up of all different types of people, we need to pay attention to how others might see something.

Knowing how perception works can help stop miscommunication and misunderstanding, like when we get upset with others because they don't see things the way we do. The fact is, they don't. They can't. No one can see things like you do except you.

SEEING THROUGH OUR SUBCONSCIOUS FILTERS

Since we all see things through perceptual filters, we must recognize and overcome these filters to get a more accurate picture of the world around us. We can do that the same way we can improve our active observation skills: with practice.

Every bit of information, whether we sense it or not, passes through our brains. And we can strengthen or rewire those pathways just by thinking! To test just how powerful our brains are, experimenters at the Cleveland Clinic in Ohio asked people to mentally exercise their fingers without actually moving them. After imagining a hand workout for fifteen minutes a day for twelve weeks,

people actually increased their finger muscle strength by 35 percent. They did this just by thinking about it![27] The muscle gain without moving was possible because the mental rehearsal of movement activates the same cortical areas of the brain as physical movement.

We can work on our own perceptual filters simply by understanding that they exist, which happens as soon as we pay attention to them.[28] The moment we become aware of something we haven't thought about before, it crosses into our consciousness. Once we are aware of these filters, we can address them, sort through them, and overcome them if necessary.

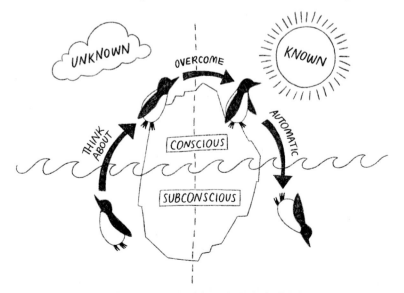

Eventually this process will become almost automatic. We will be able to look *through* our perceptive filters without even thinking about it. Remember how you learned to tie your shoes. At first you really had to concentrate on the process, but after some practice it became an action you could do unconsciously—probably even with your eyes closed.

Let's examine some of our own personal perceptual filters by studying this sculpture:

How does it make you feel?

There's no right or wrong answer; we all feel how we feel.

How would you feel if you saw someone defacing it with spray paint?

How would you feel if you saw someone crying next to it?

Is the statue missing anything?

How we feel about something is shaped by our personal experiences, which then activate our perceptual filters. To uncover your filters, mentally check off the following questions if you answer yes.

Does the statue remind you of . . .
- A time you were sad?
- A time you were lonely?
- A time you were hungry?
- A time you were afraid?
- A time you felt left out?
- A time someone close to you was sad, lonely, hungry, afraid, or excluded?

Does the statue remind you of . . .
- Anyone in your life?
- Anyone in your town?
- A rich person?
- A poor person?
- Anyone from a TV show you've watched?

Where we come from, where we are in that moment, and where we want to be in the future all affect how we see things. What we see is also colored by many things, including our mood, the people around us, and what we've read or seen.

Along with thinking about what filters we may have, think about what filters others might have. Show the photo to someone else and ask them the same questions from page 50.

Learning how other people deal with information can help us discover things we missed the first time. For instance, I never thought about the statue missing shoes until someone else pointed it out to me. I've always been lucky enough to have shoes, so whenever I go barefoot, it's for fun. Thinking about the reasons someone might not own shoes changed the way I saw the entire sculpture.

To gather the most information possible, don't close your eyes to anything, even someone else's filters.

THE MOST COMMON PERCEPTUAL FILTERS

There are three very common perceptual filters we should always be on the lookout for, in ourselves and in others:

1. Seeing What We *Want* to See
2. Seeing What We're *Told* to See
3. Not Seeing *Change*

SEEING WHAT WE WANT TO SEE

The scientific terms for seeing what we want to see include wishful seeing, confirmation bias, and tunnel vision.[29] Even if we don't realize it, our brains will look for things that support what we're already expecting to see and to ignore things that don't fit in with our initial ideas.

We can see proof of this in ourselves in something called frequency illusion. Frequency illusion is when you first hear about something and then suddenly see it everywhere.[30] For instance, when you see an ad for new sneakers and then notice them on a lot of people's feet. Everyone didn't just run out and buy the shoes because they saw the ad when you did. They already had them; you just didn't notice.

By the end of this book, the same thing is likely to happen with the way you notice art. After being asked to pay close attention to so many different works of art, you might start to see images of art everywhere: on cereal boxes, umbrellas, bumper stickers, and laptop covers. Artwork won't have mysteriously increased in the world. The images were always there. You'll only start to notice them because they line up with your new observation skills, and you've stopped blocking them out.

Wishful Seeing: seeing something because you want to see it so badly. For instance, when people are shown footage of a football player possibly stepping out of bounds, fans of the player's team are more likely to see his foot as in bounds, while fans of the opposing team are more likely to see it as out.[31]

Confirmation Bias: the tendency to look for things that support what we already think. For instance, if a dog bit a child, someone who loves animals might see it as a harmless nip caused by the child aggravating the dog, while someone who is afraid of dogs might see the same incident as a dangerous attack on an innocent child.[32]

Tunnel Vision: focusing on only one thing because we've decided it's important and ignoring everything else. For instance, a person nearing victory in a video game might pay such close attention to the TV that they don't even see their little sister chasing the cat behind it.[33]

FEELING FREQUENCY ILLUSION

Painted in 1917 by Childe Hassam, THE AVENUE IN THE RAIN is now owned by the White House in Washington, DC. Look closely at the American flags. Now notice how many times you see an American flag over the next few days.

Our wishful seeing can change the importance and frequency of how we see things, but it can also change an object's physical appearance to us.[34] In experiments around the world, researchers have found that our desires make things seem physically larger or closer than they really are. In the Netherlands, subjects were asked to guess the size of a chocolate muffin. People on a diet estimated the muffin was much bigger than non-dieters did because it was something they were craving.[35] In New York, subjects were shown a water bottle and asked how close it was to them. Thirsty participants reported that the beverage was closer to them than the non-thirsty ones did.[36]

While the tendency to see what we want to believe is largely unconscious, we can reduce its effect simply by knowing it exists. To make sure you aren't mistaking your desires for facts, ask yourself two questions:

Is what I'm seeing what I thought I'd see?

and

Does seeing it this way help me at all?

If you answer yes to either of these questions, you might be experiencing wishful seeing, so take a step back and look again.

SEEING WHAT WE'RE TOLD TO SEE

Sometimes other people can add perceptual filters to our own observations because we look for what we think others want us to find.

If before showing you *The Collective* (the propane tank sculpture of a head), I revealed that local residents hated it and were petitioning the city to have it removed, you might have been quicker to determine it was "ugly" or paid more attention to the rust.

To overcome this, pay special attention to any outside suggestions or restrictions that might be placed on your observation skills.

Look at the following work by James Rosenquist. It's called *White Paint.*

Can you imagine what it smells like?

Can you imagine what it feels like?

Can you imagine eating it?

If you can't imagine eating it, why not?

If you're not supposed to think about eating it, why did the artist include a red-handled spatula in the bowl?

What do spatulas like that remind you of?

Oh, I'm sorry, I got the title wrong. It's not *White Paint*; it's called *White Frosting*. Does knowing that change any of your answers? Would it smell different? Would you eat it now?

If you were thinking that there's paint in the bowl, even though your eyes were telling you it looked a little thicker and fluffier than paint, it's probably because I told you the title was *White Paint*. You ignored your eyes and your brain because of what I told you to see. To find the facts, don't throw away what you know to be true just to please someone else.

NOT SEEING CHANGE

Another common perceptual filter is that we don't always notice changes even if they happen right in front of our eyes. It isn't that surprising since our brains encounter *eleven million bits of information each second.*[37] But when we forget that things are constantly changing, we can miss important details, or worse, go into autopilot.

When anyone says, "I've seen this before," they're wrong. They may have seen or handled similar things, but not what's new in front of them—that one has never existed before.

Imagine you took a photograph of the same tree every single day for a year. How much would those pictures change? It might always be the same tree, but the weather, the other plants around it, and the light won't ever be exactly the same. The ladybug climbing up its bark has never gone exactly the same way with exactly the same steps at exactly the same time ever before.

No two classrooms, friends, customers, students, patients, people, or problems are the same. Every person and situation is unique. And we need to approach them that way.

We all have unconscious filters that can keep us from seeing the best way, the most useful way, or the truth. Once we're aware of our personal perceptual filters though, we can see past them . . . even the stuff that is hiding right in front of us.

CHAPTER 4

WINNING AT HIDE-AND-SEEK

OUR PERCEPTUAL FILTERS CAN BLOCK OR COLOR WHAT we see, but they can also lead us into dangerous territory. Sometimes they cause our brains to treat assumptions as facts—which isn't good for anyone.

Do you know who this is?

Even if you aren't a huge sports fan, you can probably figure out from the photograph that the person is a professional basketball player who played for the Los Angeles Lakers. You can also see that he is a Black man, and he is tall.

What else can you tell about him besides his sports history? You can see he is bald. He has muscular arms. He's wearing a white cuff on his right wrist. He

has on clear, protective glasses. And he's looking up while holding a basketball. But from this photograph, we can't tell much else.

Let's play a game called Three Truths and a Lie. I'll give you four statements about the man. Only three of them are true. Can you spot the lie?

- He won six National Basketball Association (NBA) championships.
- He has two million followers on Instagram.
- He has a doctorate from Princeton University.
- He's had houses in New York, California, and Hawaii.

Without more concrete information, most people will guess based on their assumptions. They'll choose what they think is true based on what is usually true for professional athletes: that famous basketball stars generally have a lot of money and a lot of fans. So, the Instagram followers and multiple houses seem possible. Since he is tall and wearing a Lakers jersey, he was probably a good player and the Lakers are a winning team, so his having won six NBA championships seems likely as well. Professional athletes are not known for their education or their interest in the sciences, so people may guess that he does not have a doctorate from Princeton University.

Those people are wrong.

The man in the above photograph is Kareem Abdul-Jabbar. He is seven feet and two inches tall, and he is a basketball legend. He played in the NBA for twenty seasons from 1969 to 1989 for the Milwaukee Bucks and then the Los Angeles Lakers. He won six NBA championships, was the season MVP six times as well, and is the league's all-time leading scorer. However, to assume he is just an athlete would be to miss out on all his other extraordinary achievements. He's also a cancer activist, US Cultural Ambassador, and best-selling author of fourteen books, including the Mycroft Holmes series about Sherlock's older brother. He graduated from UCLA with a degree in history and holds an honorary doctorate from Princeton University.* His kids' book *What Color Is My World?* is about the lost history of African-American inventors. Abdul-Jabbar is an innovator who works to bring science, sports, and history together.[38]

KAREEM & SHERLOCK

Kareem was in his twenties when he got his first set of Sherlock Holmes books, right before his first road trip with the Milwaukee Bucks.[39] He read the series on the beach and fell in love.

"I was fascinated by Holmes's ability to see clues where other people saw nothing," he said. "It was like he saw the world in color while everyone else saw in black and white."

Kareem wanted to see life in color as well, so he worked on sharpening his observation skills— skills that quickly helped him on the basketball court. He would study the body language and posture of the other players, looking

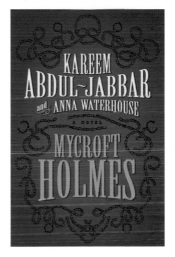

for clues he could use to defeat them. He paid attention to what other people missed. During one game, he heard the ball boys talking about how a player on the other team smoked in the locker room at halftime. Kareem used that information to change his own playing strategy.

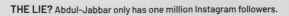

THE LIE? Abdul-Jabbar only has one million Instagram followers.

"I knew, if [he] was smoking, if I made him run in the second half he'd be in pain," he recalls. "Sure enough, he got too winded to play. We won the game."

In 2015, Kareem took his Sherlock fandom to another level and released *Mycroft Holmes*, the first book in a mystery series revolving around Sherlock's older, smarter, and lazier brother.

Let's explore some more of our assumptions. Take a look at these two images:

List five things that are different and five things that are the same about them.

Did you include that they seem to be different ages?

Which one do you think is younger?

The image on the left is the younger one; it shows a twenty-year-old man. The image on the right is of a twenty-four-year-old man. Did you get it right? If not, what made you think the man on the left was older?

Did you note that they are different people? They are not. They are the same man. Each is a self-portrait painted by Pablo Picasso.

🧠 🧠 🧠 🧠

To accurately gather information from what we observe, we cannot assume anything. Appearances can be deceiving. Assumptions can mean we miss the correct information.

How can we avoid making assumptions? By approaching each situation with an open mind, looking past the obvious, and focusing only on what we can observe to be true, not what we assume it to be.

If we want to learn the truth and not rely on lies, we need to concentrate on collecting *all* the facts. To do this, we'll use the same basic model of information gathering that the FBI, journalists, and scientific researchers use: we'll look for the *who, what, where, when,* and *why.*

Who is involved? What happened? When did it happen? Where did the action take place? And why did it happen?

Let's start with the image on the right:

WHO?

Who is the subject of this scene?

Most people tell me it's a woman. How can we tell? The figure is wearing a dress and seems to have long black hair held up by flowers. The person's eyes and mouth are small. We can't verify right now that it's a woman, but we don't want to leave the figure undescribed. In that case, we'll use the words "appears to be" or "seems" to signal that this is our best guess but not a firm fact. So, the best answer right now is: the picture appears to be a woman.

Is the woman the only figure in the painting?

There isn't another person, but there is another being: a horse. Do you see it peeking over her head? Good.

What else do we know about the figure? Do we know their name? Not yet. There does appear to be a character-based language printed on the upper-right side and bottom center of the print. Maybe those are clues that will give us a name or more information about the work. We'll note that and see if we can find someone to translate it for us.

What is the figure wearing? A dress? Be more specific. If you had to describe this individual to someone else, how would you do it? They are wearing a blue-and-red long-sleeve dress with red ruffled cuffs printed with a floral pattern. The dress has layers and many ornate details, like buckles around the ankles, so it might be a traditional or ceremonial outfit. Looking closer, it seems like there is a square of fabric tied around the figure's middle with a belt featuring hanging charms.

What else can we observe about their attire? They are wearing blue-and-brown shoes with buckles. They have flowers in their hair but no other type of hat. Their hands are uncovered, and they have a sword in each of them.

What about the figure's body position? They seem to be in an odd position. Their face points one way, but their feet point in the opposite direction. At first glance, it looks like they are facing us, but if we stand up and place our feet in the same position and then move our head to the right, it becomes clearer that we're looking at their back. They are twisting backward, like Neo dodging bullets in the movie *The Matrix*. In fact, we now notice all the arrows flying around them. Perhaps they are twisting away from them.

Objectively assessing what a person is wearing, how they're behaving, and how they're interacting with the objects around them can help us uncover their identity.

WHAT?

The second question is *what* happened or what's happening. What is the main action?

In this image, there is a lot going on. The figure is twisting back, dodging arrows. A lot of arrows. All aimed at them.

How many arrows are there?

Since arrows are usually shot only one at a time, there's probably many people shooting at them. On the horse behind the person, we can see part of an elaborate saddle and headpiece on it. If the horse were bare and the individual holding flowers, we could probably say they didn't expect to be attacked. The fact that they are holding two swords tells us they were most likely expecting a fight of some kind.

WHERE?

Now let's investigate *where*. Where is the scene taking place?

Is it indoors or outdoors? How do you know?

There is a tree, and the ground is green. It is outdoors.

What country do you think it is in?

The person looks like they might be Asian, so we'll start there. Their dress reminds me of a kimono, which are most often worn in Japan but are worn other places as well. A Google search of the characters on the image confirms that they are Japanese. The scene appears to be set in Japan.

WHEN?

Finally, we need to assess *when*. What facts can we find about when this scene occurred?

What time of year is it?

The figure's long sleeves suggest that it is not blazing hot. The tree has tiny leaf buds, which means it might be spring.

What time of day is it?

The fact that the image is outside and is bright without any artificial lights around tells us it is daytime. In Japan, in early spring, the sun rises at 6:00 a.m. and sets by 6:00 p.m., so we have a twelve-hour window. There are no signs of a sunrise or sunset. This suggests the time is somewhere between 9:00 a.m. and 4:00 p.m.

At this point you might be saying, "So what? Who cares?" But the secrets of life are often revealed through small details. Small details can solve crimes. Small details can lead to significant discoveries. Small details reveal big things.

What about the year or time period? Do you think the image is set in the past, present, or future? What is your evidence?

The figure's dress does not look modern, unless it's being worn for a holiday. The fact that they are using a horse for transportation also points us to the past. The swords and arrows are the biggest clue since they are not weapons used today.

I'm not an expert on Japanese art, but I can find one. My source tells me that this image is a woodblock print in the *ukiyo-e* (pronounced "ew-key-YO-yay") style, which was popular in Japan from the seventeenth through the nineteenth centuries. At first they were only done with black outlines, but color was added during the eighteenth century.

A Utagawa Kuniyoshi woodblock print

I can also ask someone familiar with Japanese history about the style of clothes the figure is wearing and find out that the dress is not a Japanese kimono but a Chinese Han silk robe! So perhaps the setting is not Japan after all. . . . Looking up famous Japanese *ukiyo-e* artists in the eighteenth century, I come upon Utagawa Kuniyoshi, whose other works look similar to this one, especially in the features of the figure's face. I learn that Kuniyoshi painted many different things—landscapes, women, cats—but was also famous for his drawings of legendary heroes, both Japanese and Chinese. Looking for an Asian hero who wielded two swords, I find Hu Sanniang. With this information, I can confirm that the print is of Hu Sanniang, a mythical Chinese heroine, done by Japanese artist Utagawa Kuniyoshi sometime between 1822 and 1835 as part of his series 108 Heroes of the Popular Water Margin.

WHY?

Our final question is the one you've probably been asking since you were born: why? *Why is the sky blue?* (Because blue light travels in smaller, shorter waves than the other colors, we see it more easily and more often in the sky when all the colors from the sun enter the Earth's atmosphere.[40]) *Why don't cats have belly buttons?* (Since they're mammals like us, cats do; theirs are just harder to see under all that fur.[41]) *Why do I have to eat broccoli?* (It packs one of the best nutritional punches of any vegetable since it's high in fiber, boosts your immune system to protect you from getting sick, and can even prevent cancer![42])

BELLY BUTTON WHYS

Why Do Humans Have Belly Buttons Anyway?

Instead of laying eggs, all mammals, including humans, grow babies inside

the female. A tube called the umbilical cord runs between the female and the baby to deliver oxygen and nutrients. For humans, after birth, the umbilical cord is cut, leaving behind baby's first scar: the belly button (also called a navel or the umbilicus by doctors).[43] Once you're out in the world, the belly button serves no real purpose, except perhaps to prove that you're not a robot.

Why Are Some Human Belly Buttons Innies and Some Outies?
Many people think it's because of how their doctor cut off their umbilical cord, but the truth is, whether you have a belly button that sticks out or sinks in is based on how much space you have between your skin and muscle wall. Only 10 percent of humans have an outie belly button![44]

If you've ever been told not to ask "why," ask "why not?" "Why?" is one of the best ways to uncover information, and far too many people forget to ask it. When your teacher walks into class frowning and throws down a pop quiz, instead of just assuming he likes to make students squirm, ask yourself why. Maybe his car broke down or his dog is sick or he's under pressure to cover more chapters. Ask him why. "Why don't you look happy today?"

Asking why might have helped Sir Arthur Conan Doyle realize that his professor would make a great fictional character. Why were Dr. Bell's classes always so full? Because people loved to listen to him solve medical mysteries—the perfect setup for a popular detective series.

In Springfield, Missouri, students at Kickapoo High School, named for the tribe that used to live in the area, asked why they were all still wearing feather headdresses for school spirit and cheering on a "chief" mascot when it was 2021 and the majority of them weren't of Native American descent. They were told it was part of the history of the school and meant to honor the Native American tribe. The students, however, felt that it had become offensive. Kickapoo Tribal Chairman Lester Randall agreed: "Native American names, symbols or images for use as a mascot, logo or team name is derogatory and has serious psychological, social and cultural consequences for Native Americans, and specifically Native Youth."[45]

To draw attention to their cause, the students started a petition at Change.org. Kickapoo High's principal Bill Powers said that in his entire time at the school, no one had ever questioned the traditions.[46] Asking why was the first step for the students to usher in change.

School leaders and administrators met with students who supported the change, a group of alumni who didn't, and the local tribe. "Just listening to both sides," Powers said, "we felt like there were some things we could do better."[47]

Seven months later, those things were on display at Kickapoo High's first home football game. The school's nickname was still the Chiefs, but the logo was changed, there was no feathered mascot, and the teepee that players used to run through was gone. It turns out the old traditions weren't just culturally insensitive; they were also historically inaccurate since the local Kickapoo tribe didn't wear feather headdresses or live in teepees. "We did learn some things and we want to learn more," Powers concluded.[48]

To learn more about the artwork on page 63, there are several whys we can ask. Why is the young woman being attacked by arrows? Why did a Japanese artist create such a detailed print of a Chinese warrior? In this case, there is nothing in the picture that will give us the answers, but it doesn't matter. What's important is that we asked the questions. By doing so, we've brought them to light so no one can say, "Well, nobody ever questioned this." And maybe the next person to come along will have the answers.

AVENGERS ASSEMBLE!

We do not know what battle Hu Sanniang was in, where she came from or is going, or how she feels. We will never have all the answers—not many people do—but the more observant we can be, the more facts we can collect, catalog, and process, the more accurate the information we will be able to uncover.

Six hundred years before the Avengers or the Justice League, a Chinese author, thought by many to be the writer Shi Nai'an, wrote a tale about 108 extraordinary heroes who banded together to protect their country. The story, called *Water Margin*, or *Outlaws of the Marsh*, is now known as one of the "Four Great Classical Novels" of Chinese literature. One of these was a female hero who might have inspired Wonder Woman. Called Hu Sanniang, she was a beautiful and formidable warrior who could dance on her horse while riding it, fought with two swords at once, and trapped bad guys with her magical red lasso.

In investigating an image we've never seen before, we learned about Japanese woodblock printing, Chinese literature, and that DC Comics' Wonder Woman might have been inspired by the tale of 108 outlaws. For every fact we uncovered, we learned something new that opened a door to something else. These doors might just lead you to your Big Idea, your life's passion, or the thing that will make you the happiest. Never stop looking and learning, for you never know what might come of it!

SEEING WHAT'S HIDING IN PLAIN SIGHT

Meet Mrs. Winthrop or, as I like to call her, Hannah. You can visit her "in person" at The Metropolitan Museum of Art in New York City.[49] Hannah's portrait was painted by John Singleton Copley in 1773. Take a few minutes to observe as much as you can about the who, what, where, and when of this scene.

Did you observe . . .

- ☑ The bright shade of blue of her dress
- ☑ Her double white lace cuffs
- ☒ The blue, black, and white striped bow on her chest
- ☑ The red, black, and white striped bow on her cap
- ☑ Her brown hair
- ☒ The string of pearls around her neck
- ☑ The red seat behind her back
- ☑ Her dimples
- ☑ The wrinkles under her eyes
- ☑ The ring on her left ring finger
- ☑ The nectarine she holds in her right hand
- ☑ The small stem with a leaf and nectarine still attached in her left hand

No one is going to see everything at first. Most people will miss some of the small details. They see the cuffs but don't notice there are two layers of lace. But what is more surprising is that so many people miss the big details staring them in the face. I have one more question for you:

Did you see the wooden table at which she is sitting?

The table is an important detail because it's what this painting is famous for: how accurately the artist was able to capture the woman's reflection in the table. And it's quite large. The table takes up almost the bottom third of the painting. It seems impossible that we could miss something so large, yet most of us do. In countless situations big and small, we overlook the "wooden table," and in doing so, miss a crucial piece of information that is hiding in plain sight.

Have you ever searched the refrigerator for mayonnaise or ketchup and couldn't find it only to have your mom pop over and grab it instantly? My mom used to say, "If it were a snake, it would have bitten you." It happens to so many of us so often that it even has a nickname: refrigerator blindness.[50] How can we miss things that are staring us in the face? Because we're wired to.

BIOLOGICALLY "BLIND"

WHAT IS THIS A PHOTO OF?

Sometimes, for no good reason, we fail to see something that's in our direct line of sight, like our jacket or the mayonnaise.[51] Scientists call this inattentional blindness. We overlook things when they are too familiar or when they blend in. However, our blind spots don't mean that our visual processing system doesn't work. Instead, they are proof of our brain's remarkable efficiency.

While the world is filled with limitless information and stimulation, our brain cannot, and should not, process everything we see. If it did, we would be overwhelmed. Imagine standing in the

 INATTENTIONAL BLINDNESS: the psychological phenomenon of not seeing something right in front of us because we are paying attention to a different detail and our brains can process only so much information at once.

middle of an amusement park like Walt Disney World. Our eyes would encounter thousands of physical things all at once—dozens of trees and buildings, flagpoles, trolleys, shops, signs, strollers, street performers, and some of the fifty thousand people who visit the park every day—but we do not "see" it all.[52] Our brain automatically filters our surroundings and allows only a small percentage of information to pass through to protect us from an information overload that might otherwise paralyze us.

Did you see the hidden person lying in the rocks? Johannes Stötter is famous for his body painting art.

Think about what our brain manages as we walk down the street in Disney World. Our body is navigating the pavement and steering us around potential obstacles (watch out for that trash can!); we are headed in a certain direction (toward Splash Mountain); we are noticing people and landmarks as we pass them (the sign said ADVENTURELAND); we might be talking or listening to another person; and we do it all effortlessly. We are able to do this only because our brain has filtered out the unnecessary: the ants on the sidewalk, the breeze blowing through the branches, the crumbs on the mustache of the man who just passed us. If we paid attention to every piece of information in our path, we wouldn't get very far.

The process of sorting out the important information from the giant amount being thrown at us is done quickly, involuntarily, and somewhat unconsciously. Our brain scans our environment until something captures its attention; only then is it uploaded into our thoughts. All the extra information passes through the brain unnoticed. Of course, our failure to see something doesn't mean it doesn't exist. The cowboy bear playing a guitar on the sidewalk is there whether we "saw" him or not.

FILLING IN THE _____

The ability to filter information also allows us to focus. Without it, we might not have survived as a species.[53] If a prehistoric hunter had to hide in the tall grass waiting for a gazelle to wander by and he was mesmerized by every swaying blade, dinner might never be served. Being able to zoom in and focus on certain objects or data in the middle of our chaotic world is why we can carry on a conversation in a crowded restaurant, or ride a bike while singing a song, or play a sport in front of a screaming crowd. In our daily lives, we usually only see what's important in our current situation, and we do it so quickly that we hardly notice the process.

This instant organization of data is only possible because our brains are built to automatically fill in the gaps for us.[54] The fact that we cna stlil reda wrods wtih jumbeld lettres and whn vwls r mssng proves this.[55]

Our friend the hunter might be ignoring the grass and focusing on a gazelle that just wandered into his line of sight, but that doesn't mean his brain wouldn't notice a heavy rustling sound nearby. The sound alone could cause the hunter to run without thinking, without even making sure there was a predator close to him, and save his life. The knowledge that the rustling might mean a lion is within walking distance is filled in automatically by his brain, which doesn't wait for permission before sending RUN! instructions.

Want to see some more examples of how your magical brain can fill in the gaps? Read the following sentence just once, and count all the Fs as you go:

CHEF FABIO FABBI BAKED DOZENS
OF DONUTS OF DIFFERENT
KINDS EVEN THOUGH HE
WASN'T FOND OF CHOCO-
LATE DESSERTS HIMSELF.

How many Fs are there?

How many did you get? Eight? Nine? There are ten Fs in the sentence.

While some of you might have gotten it correct, most of us wouldn't because our quick-thinking brains would fill in a V for the F in words like "of" since that's the sound the letter is making.

Let's try another one. Look at these two photographs of a dog. The top one is black-and-white, yes? No colors at all. Underneath it is a very colorful photo of the same dog with lots of oranges and purples.

Now we're going to see the brain in action. Focus your eyes on the red dot in the center of the bottom colorful photo for thirty seconds, then quickly look back up at the black-and-white image.

What did you see? Did the top black-and-white photo suddenly turn to color? And were they the correct colors—the grass was green, the sky was blue?

What you saw is called a negative afterimage, and it happened because the part of your eye that sees light got tired.[56] Our eyes are used to moving around thousands of times a day, not staring at one spot. This sudden stop made the cone cells in your eyes (which interpret color) shut down a bit and send weaker signals to the brain about what colors you were looking at. When you looked at the new image, your brain, for a brief second, filled in the opposite colors from what you had been staring at, so purple became green and orange became blue. It was a tiny, temporary glitch, but it shows how our visual processing system does things without our knowledge.

Our brain's ability to fill in the gaps for us can sometimes save our life, like with the hunter in the grass. But we have to remember that we don't always see things perfectly, and we don't perceive it all. While missing the Fs in a sentence might not seem like a crucial problem, sometimes what we fail to see is.

Small details make a big difference. There is a huge difference between class starting at 9:30 a.m. instead of 10:30 a.m., between that new app costing $3.99 and $3.99 a month, between one teaspoon of salt and one tablespoon. Missing important details can cause a catastrophe (and really hard-to-eat cookies).

Finding and focusing on the details doesn't just help avoid disaster though; it can also lead to a solution. Think of the billion-dollar companies built on their attention to detail. Apple didn't get its reputation for beautiful phones, tablets, and watches by accident. The company paid attention to every detail, from the design to the box-opening experience.[57]

When Walt Disney was working on a new form of robotic animation called Audio-Animatronics®, his engineers told him it would be difficult to have the figures move when they weren't in the spotlight.[58] Disney, however, insisted that the Tiki birds and presidents must realistically breathe and shuffle even when they weren't speaking. This attention to detail helped make The Walt Disney Company one of the largest media companies in the world.

It's not a coincidence that Virgin Atlantic airline, ranked by many as the best in customer satisfaction, advertises on its website "We get all the details just right."[59]

Mastering the details will give you a competitive edge. Thoroughness and thoughtfulness aren't important to everyone, so if you make them a priority, they can help you stand out from the crowd of people who don't bother to notice them.

DETAIL-ORIENTED

The more attuned we are to the details, the more we will see them. To help us learn to see the wooden table hiding in plain sight, let's go back and look at it. Turn to page 72 and study the table at which Mrs. Winthrop is sitting. What specifics on and around the table can you point out that you might not have noticed before?

Do you now see . . .

☑ That the tabletop is shiny?

☑ The light reflected along the raised edge at the bottom-left corner of the table?

☑ The reflection of Mrs. Winthrop?

Look closely at Mrs. Winthrop's hands. She was married to a Harvard professor. We can see her wedding ring on her left ring finger; however, if you look at that hand in the reflection on the table you will find that the ring is missing!

If we had missed the wooden table the first time around, we would have missed the vanishing wedding ring as well. And it's a crucial detail not to be missed, since the artist Copley cared so much about creating the reflection in the table, he would not likely leave out such an item accidentally. There are no records of why the ring is missing in the reflection. We don't need to know the importance of the missing ring to note that it's missing. If we don't point out that detail, we could be leaving out critical information we'll need later on. You never know when that one small detail will crack the case or change everything.

While it's in our biology to miss things, we can consciously make sure details aren't slipping through our filters unnoticed. Training our brains to be more effective at observation and perception will not only help us see more but also miss less.

Look around you, your house, your school, your favorite park and ask yourself: What is hiding in plain sight?

🧠 🧠 🧠 🧠

Now that we've mastered the fine art of observation and have learned *how* to see, we're going to learn how to *think* about what we see.

How to **THINK**
About What You See

"IF EVERYONE IS THINKING ALIKE,
THEN NO ONE IS THINKING."

—Benjamin Franklin

CHAPTER 5

THE PLAYGROUND MADE YOU SMARTER

ONE OF THE BEST-SELLING AUTHORS OF ALL TIME SAID the secret to his success is rooted in a simple motto: "Change the way you look at things, and the things you look at change." [60] How we look at things, our point of view, is called perspective, and we need to keep changing it to find the most information.

For instance, where we stand when we view something can change the way we see it, so it's important that we consider objects and situations from every possible physical angle. Search behind things, underneath them, in the corners, and off the page. Step back, crouch down, and walk around. Things are not always what they appear to be, especially at first glance from only one angle. Let's examine this bowl of food.

Write down what you see.

I saw an onion, carrots, mushrooms, a turnip, parsnips, garlic, a sprig of mint, a few different kinds of lettuce, and a furry thing near the middle left that I had to look up (it's a chestnut). Everything is in a dark bowl that appears to be made of some type of reflective metal and rests on a flat surface.

Did you see the *man* in the image? Go back and look again. Come back here when you find it or give up.

When you flip the painting upside down, there he is:

From a different angle, the image changes entirely. Instead of the ingredients for a salad, we now have the outline of a person.[61] If we had originally looked at the image from every angle, including sideways or upside down, we would have seen it.

When was the last time you hung upside down? For most of us, it was probably at the playground. Think of how you explore a playground. You climb up and over and under things. You hang upside down and sideways and spin. You follow paths and then make your own, like trying to figure out how to climb the outside of a structure, rather than just walking up the steps. You see strangers sliding down the slides or swinging along the monkey bars as potential playmates, but you still keep an eye on your mom or aunt or grandparent sitting on the park bench.

To get the most thorough perspective, explore the world the way you do on the playground. Discover every bit of it, even what's hiding along the edges. Change your position. Invent new ones. Be brave, be bold, be loud! View other people as potential friends, but never forget about your own safety. Bring the same outgoing, adventurous spirit that fills you with wonder and joy at the playground or at school or on a trip to the rest of your life. With open eyes, an open mind, and an open heart, there is no end to what you can uncover.

HIDDEN PERSPECTIVES

Perspective, however, isn't always easy to see.

List all the objects you see in the painting *The Ambassadors* by Hans Holbein the Younger, that follows.

There's a table with a red carpet on top, two globes, a sundial, a lute (the stringed instrument), a bag of flutes, three books, and a giant skull. Did you see the skull? It's almost as big as the men in the painting.

To see it in the bottom center of the work, hold this book up in front of your face and slowly twist it clockwise until the edge of the page is lined up with your right eye. Do you see it? Keep trying until you're able to find the correct perspective that reveals a skull, like so:

Now turn back to the first image in this section, of people in a room with green-striped walls on page 83, and see if you can find the hidden object. Come back here when you're done.

The painting is called *School of Beauty, School of Culture,* and was created by Kerry James Marshall, whose work also appears in Chapter 1. If you hold this book up and turn it clockwise again, a blond Disney-like princess emerges.

Holbein put the skull into his painting to remind viewers that they should make the most of their lives. But what about Marshall? What do you think he was trying to get viewers to notice? Let's study the different perspectives in the painting to find out.

First, like good detectives-in-training, we'll cover the basics: who, what, where, when, and why this scene is taking place.

WHO?

How many people are in the painting? Count carefully, as some of those seen in mirrors are not the same person sitting in front of them due to the angle. (For instance, the person bending down in front of the floor-length mirror in the center is not the same person as the one taking a flash photograph.) How many did you find?

I counted fourteen people in the painting—twelve adults and two children. Ten of the people appear to be women based on their clothes, shoes, and body shapes, and three appear to be men; however, this cannot be confirmed. The face of the photographer in the mirror is hidden by the camera, so that person's gender is unknown. Additionally, there are five people who appear to be women featured in posters on the walls.

All the people in the painting, even in the advertisements, are Black, except for the hidden blond girl.

WHAT?

What is going on in the painting? People are sitting, standing, bending, posing, talking, taking photographs, and getting their hair or makeup done. One of the children is drinking from a yellow bottle or a sippy cup, while the other is squatting to investigate the crooked image of the blond girl.

WHERE?

Where does the painting take place? A salon. We can see the name of the salon printed in English reflected in the mirror: SCHOOL and SCHOOL OF CULTURE. The posters also have English words on them: "dark," "lovely," and "tate." There are three horizontal color stripes behind the beauty salon name—red, black, and green. The stripes are featured in that order on the Pan-African flag, often used by Black Americans to represent their culture. The salon is likely located in the United States. A quick Google search confirms that there is a real-life Your School of Beauty Culture in Chicago, right around the corner from one of Marshall's first studios.[62]

WHEN?

When does this scene take place? The poster on the far right seems to have more writing on it, so let's zoom in:

What can you read? I see the word "TATE" in capital letters, which might refer to the Tate, which is a museum in London, and a range of dates: January 27–May 16, 2010. Researching this, we can find that the Tate held an exhibit during those dates featuring the work of artist

Chris Ofili, an artist known for paintings that frequently feature Black women. Therefore, the Marshall painting must take place some time after 2010.

WHY?

We're now left with the most important question about Marshall's painting: Why would he paint a White girl in the middle of a salon filled with Black stylists and customers?

To figure it out, let's give her a who-what-where-when-why workup.

Who is she? We can only see her head and a bit of her clothing, but from her facial structure, eyelashes, and hair, she does appear to be a young woman. She has very light white- and peach-colored skin and bright yellow hair. We can't see the color of her eyes. She's wearing a red top with a white collar.

How does she compare with the other people in the painting? She is the only one with white skin. She is the only one with blond hair. Does anyone else have the same hairstyle: long, flowing, wavy curls? No. How many different hairstyles can you spot on the people in the salon, in person, and in the posters on the wall?

What is she? She's a symbol meant to represent something. Even though she's partially hidden by the angle, we know from *The Ambassadors* that artists used this slanted technique on purpose to draw extra attention to something.

Having seen many classic Disney films, I instantly recognized her similarity with the fictional character Princess Aurora, aka Briar Rose, from the 1959 animated feature *Sleeping Beauty*. Aurora does wear a dress with a white collar and a red cloak while walking in the woods. She is popular and well-known around the world as her castle is the centerpiece of Disneyland, Disneyland Park Paris, and Hong Kong Disneyland when it first opened.

What is she doing? Nothing. She's just hovering. She's there; she exists; she even casts a shadow on the ground,* but she's not interacting with any of the people in the painting. In fact, she seems kind of removed from everything else that is going on.

Where is she? She's floating in the middle of the salon, near the bottom of the painting. Although she's tilted, she's not hidden. Her neon yellow hair makes her stand out immediately. You might not have seen her full face right away, but unlike in the skull painting, you probably noticed her. The little boy in the blue overalls certainly does. He's looking behind her, maybe trying to figure out what's going on, who she is,

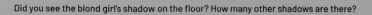

* Did you see the blond girl's shadow on the floor? How many other shadows are there?

and what she's doing there. The little girl in pink, footed pajamas seems to be pointing to her as well. The adults in the painting, however, ignore the blond image. Do they know she's there? If so, it seems as if they are ignoring her completely.

When is she? Unlike the present-day setting of the salon, the blond princess is from the past. The movie character she resembles is from 1959, and her style—heavy bangs and buttoned-up collar—is not current.

Why is she here? The Disney-ish princess was put into the painting to remind viewers that there are many more types of beauty than just blond girls.[64]

DIVERSE DREAMS

How many different colors do you see? How many different shapes? How many different patterns? What cultures can you find represented?

When Hong Kong Disneyland opened in 2005, every Disney theme park was anchored by an iconic princess house—Sleeping Beauty's or, in the case of Walt Disney World and Tokyo Disneyland, Cinderella's. Fifteen years later, however, the South China Sea resort unveiled a dramatic transformation. In place of their original Sleeping Beauty castle, a new monument emerged: the Castle of Magical Dreams. Instead of representing just one European princess, the palace was redesigned to represent different cultures from around the world, including Asian, Arabic, Polynesian, Native American, Black, Celtic, and Nordic. And rather than just being the private residence of a single person, the building was dedicated to the hopes of everyone. During construction, thousands of guests were invited to write their wishes on special cards that were placed in a treasure chest and stored at the top of the tallest tower to ensure that the building would belong to all.[65]

Both Holbein and Marshall hoped that in making a viewer change their physical viewpoint, the viewer would pay more attention to how they looked at the work and at other issues in the world outside of the subject of the painting.

A SHIFT IN ATTITUDE

Changing our viewpoint can also change our attitude. The ancient Greeks purposefully carved grooves into their stone roads to make heavy wheeled carts easier for horses and oxen to pull. Once wheels were in the grooves, they gained better traction and weren't as likely to slip out and slip off the road. In the same way, our efficiency-loving brains deliberately seek familiar patterns.[66] Unfortunately, sometimes we get stuck in those ruts. Shifting our physical perspective can also help us when we're mentally mired in the mud.

Think of the last time you stared at a paper or assignment you couldn't finish. You knew what you needed to do, but the words . . . just . . . wouldn't . . . come.

Or perhaps you can't stop worrying about how well you'll do on your next test or at your next game. You obsess about it so much, you can't practice or prepare.

To help get out of that hole, take a tip from scientists: get up and go. Go for a quick walk around your house, around the hall of your school, or around the block.

"The very act of walking and moving about invigorates your brain," confirms Professor Rick Gilkey and Dr. Clint Kilts, "because the brain is an interactive system."[67] Any activity that stimulates one part of the brain such as physical movement simultaneously stimulates other parts such as creative problem-solving.

Even better than just walking is observing what you see along the way. Go on a discovery walk. Seek and sort out objective facts—who, what, where, and when. As you do this, you're allowing your brain to refocus.[68] Instead of getting caught up in thinking about the same thing, getting up and moving will engage your observational skills, which will in turn ignite your critical thinking abilities, refresh all of your senses, and in many cases release your mental block.

Mental blocks can be tough to overcome. For instance, think about the next standardized test you have to take at school. It's usually called by its initials like STEP or STAR or ISAT. There's a lot of pressure for everyone to do their best on the test. The test is usually pretty long and pretty boring. Sometimes it takes a few days to complete it.

Mental Check-in

On a scale of 1–10 . . .

How fun does the state test sound?

1 (not even a tiny bit) → 10 (super fun!)

How worried are you about it?

1 (crazy worried) → 10 (no worries here!)

How confident are you about taking it?

1 (not confident at all) → 10 (know I'll ace it!)

Now let's stop thinking about the next state test and instead get up and go somewhere. In this case, so we can stay together, we'll take a virtual nature walk through the jungle. Have you ever been to the jungle?

Jump into this next painting of the jungle from 1909. Before doing anything else, just fall into it. Let your eyes wander. Imagine you're there. Imagine you can hear the sounds and smell the smells.

Now, what do you see? Let's analyze the who, what, where, and when of this painting.

Who is in the painting?

Animals. Monkeys and a bird.

What is happening?

A bird sits on a branch in the middle of the painting surrounded by several monkeys, some of whom are eating.

When does it take place?

Near sunset or sunrise, as the sun is low in the sky.

Where is this scene?

In a jungle or a rain forest, or possibly even a zoo.

Now let's gather the details:

How many birds are there?

How many monkeys?

How many oranges?

How many flowers?

Now let's look for what might be hidden:

Do you see the blue plant?

Do you see the white plants?

Do you see the sun?

Did you see the two baby monkeys?

There are only three pink flowers and one bird, but there are twenty-three oranges and nine monkeys. Did you find them all? If you didn't, go back and search until you do.

Did you notice we missed an information-gathering question? The Why. Why is this painting significant? Because of the artist.

Henri Rousseau never went to school for art.[69] In fact, he was a tax collector! He didn't start painting until he was in his forties, and when he finally showed his works, critics made fun of them. They said his paintings were too childlike. Rousseau's work went on to become world famous, and his style was even given a name: naïve art. A single one of his paintings now sells for almost $3 million.

Even more incredibly, although he created twenty-five jungle paintings, he never saw the jungle in person. He never left his home country of France in his entire life!

LESSONS WE CAN LEARN FROM ROUSSEAU: It's never too late, don't listen to critics, and you can do anything with your imagination!

After our jungle excursion, let's get back to the state test. Did you think about it while you were searching for monkeys or imagining the sound of leaves rustling? Probably not. Your brain got a break by looking at nature and doing things it knows it's good at. Your breathing and heart rate probably slowed down, which allowed you to relax and concentrate better.

Now, what if I told you that this little exercise just helped prepare your brain for the test? It did. The test is full of large blocks of information, confusing problems, and hidden details. By training your brain to slow down and carefully observe, to look through your filters and assumptions, find similarities and differences, and discover what might be hiding right in front of you, you are prepping for that test . . . and more!

On a scale of 1–10, how confident are you about taking the state test now?

1 (not confident at all) → 10 (know I'll ace it!)

Even if your number went up only a little, think about how amazing it is that you feel more prepared just from looking at a single painting. And we're only halfway there!

USING ALL OUR SENSES

When gathering information, we must remember to use all our resources. We need to gather information from our other senses, not only our eyes.

To master this skill, purposefully try to use *all* of your senses in public and in private. When you're on the subway or at the grocery store or in your basement, note odors, and tastes, and sounds.

I find the best way to get my other senses fired up is to close my eyes for a moment. On an airplane recently, I did just that and for the first time noticed the aromas of hand lotion, perfume, and bacon. How did I possibly miss the smell of bacon on a plane when my eyes were open? We were at cruising altitude; the bacon didn't just suddenly walk on board. My eyes were commanding all my attention. I needed to turn them off so my brain would channel its resources to my other senses.

The more often you engage all your senses, the more automatic the process will become. And you'll find your nose, your ears, and even your skin will help you see. Even though it doesn't move, we can still practice this with art. We can look at a painting of a day at the beach and know what it smells like and sounds like and feels like: salty air, waves crashing, seagulls squawking, sand scraping between our toes. To prove it, we'll analyze the following painting.

Before we catalog anything, though, let's study it for a moment. What do you see? What do you think is going on?

Now let's add some sensory details.

Smell

What do you think this scene smells like?

The first thing I thought of was the smell of a barn since the image seems to show a closed place full of animals and humans. To me, barns smell like sweet hay and steamy sweat.

Can you imagine how each of the animals smells? How does the scent of a horse differ from that of a fish?

Can you find anything else that might smell?

What about the flowers? Or the garland around the horse's neck?

Touch

How do you think the rooster walking on the woman's leg feels?

Initially, I thought it would feel scratchy, but maybe it would tickle.

What would the fish feel like if you rubbed your hand against it?

How would the horse feel? Would the horse's mane feel different from the side of its body? How? Would the horse's hair feel different depending on which way you moved your hand across it?

Do you think it feels cold or hot in this scene?

With at least five creatures in the same space, I would imagine it was rather hot. The way the people are dressed—with exposed arms and legs—seems to support this.

Sound

Do you think this place is noisy or quiet? Why?

What noises do you think you might hear?

I'd expect we'd hear the rooster's drum and cymbals as well as the animal itself. We might hear the horse neighing or stomping its hooves. We would hear the violin and cello. We might hear people: the woman in red sighing or screaming or just breathing heavily; perhaps she is even singing.

MAKING SENSE OF IT ALL

By sniffing, feeling, and listening, we can collect more information and help bring a scene to life, especially one that's hard to describe. This particular blue-hued painting, though, would still be difficult to tell someone else about—unless you can find a single object hidden in plain sight. There is one item that can help us unlock the mystery of why a woman in red is twisted upside down staring at a green horse while a moon plays the violin, a chicken plays a drum, and a fish hands her flowers. Can you find it? Go back and take another peek.

Did you see it? If not, I'll give you a hint. Look just under the woman in red's legs. See it now? It's a bar supported by two lengths of wire or rope that run up toward the top of the painting— a trapeze! The woman is a trapeze artist. She isn't floating upside down unrealistically; she is doing stunts high above the ground.

Where are trapeze artists found? In the circus. The painting's artist, Marc Chagall, grew up in Russia, and traveling circuses were a big part of his childhood. He loved the dreamlike qualities of the shows: the colors, the energy, the impossible feats of human and animal performers.

As soon as we spotted the trapeze, the entire painting suddenly made sense. In real life, horses aren't green, but they can be at the circus either because of special lights or paint. Large fish don't fly through the air indoors, but remote-controlled, fish-shaped balloons can. Regular chickens don't play instruments, but trained animals or animatronic robots do.

It can be tempting to just glance at something and decide that it's "weird" or unreal. Women don't normally slither like a snake through a river in the sky. But when we look closer and see, for instance, that her knees are crossed, we can understand her position is the result of a mid-air twist, an acrobatic feat frozen in time. Once we see that, the image stops being weird and starts being wonderful.

Chagall captured multiple perspectives in his painting *Le Cirque Bleu* (French for "The Blue Circus"), but they were hard to figure out before we knew we were in the middle of a carnival. Circuses are full of lighting effects and illusions, fantastical costumes, lifelike puppets, and surprising situations. Some things, like people on stilts, are bigger than normal; others, like tiny cars, are smaller. These grand events also take place in vast arenas or tents, which means things closer to us will look larger, while those farther away will appear smaller.

The trapeze artist in red isn't the only person in the painting. How many people can you find?

Do you see the woman on the bottom right? Let's climb into her shoes to see things from her viewpoint.

What is she doing?

What do you suppose she is looking at?

Let's zoom up and survey things from an entirely different point of view: that of the fish in the top left.

How different would this scene look from above?

How would this scene smell from above?

How would this scene feel from above? Do you think it's colder or warmer at the top?

How would this scene sound from above?

Making the effort to see the world from other perspectives provides additional information to a scene or situation. But it also helps us, the viewer. In fact, the ability to imagine others' viewpoints, reactions, and concerns is one of the most important cognitive tools we humans possess.

STEPPING INTO SOMEONE ELSE'S SHOES

In *To Kill a Mockingbird*, Atticus Finch tells his daughter, Scout, "You never really understand a person until you consider things from his point of view . . . until you climb into his skin and walk around in it."[70] Seeing things from others' perspectives allows us to be more understanding and sympathetic to them, which enables us to be better friends, better teammates, and better people.

Practice inserting yourself into someone else's place both physically and mentally. What does a classroom of excited kids look like from behind the teacher's desk? What does an older sibling who is yelling look like to their younger sibling who is the one being yelled at?

Want to really step into someone else's shoes? Try switching places with your parents for an hour. Do what they do and have them pretend to be you. You'll learn a lot about the best and most challenging parts of each other's day.

PERSPECTIVE CHANGES

While looking at all the different parts of our lives, including people, places, and situations, don't forget that things change. Views change, perspectives change, opinions change.

Imagine standing in front of a window in the south of France that opened out to the clear blue waters of the Mediterranean Sea. A warm breeze blows in through the open glass. You gaze outside and it's a riot of color. At your feet on a yellow tile balcony are vibrant red, orange, and blue pots holding bunches of blossoming flowers. Dark and light green ivy twist around the balcony's black wrought-iron fence and up around the window frame. Looking beyond, you watch blue, green, and orange sailboats bobbing on sunset-pink waves under a sky swirling with long turquoise and purple clouds.

That's just what the artist Henri Matisse enjoyed for nearly a decade when he escaped the wet winters of Paris for a rented studio in the small town of Collioure. The studio's window looked out over the town's harbor. Matisse spent countless hours in front of the window painting what he saw, capturing what he called the "explosive" colors such as in this piece from 1905 simply titled *Open Window*:[71]

In 1914, he painted the exact same daytime scene, shown here.

What happened? The scene outside the window hadn't changed: it still held the bright blue Mediterranean, cheerful ships, and warm, sunny days. In fact, according to art historians, Matisse painted the trees on the balcony first and then painted black over everything.[72] What changed was the way he viewed the world.

For Matisse, life in 1914 was very different than it had been nine years earlier. World War I had recently begun, and France was suffering great casualties. The German army had invaded his hometown, trapping his mother behind enemy lines. His friends were sent off to war, his brother taken as a prisoner of war, and although Matisse had tried to join the army many times, he was told he was too old. Instead, the French military took over his house in Paris for their headquarters, and he was forced to move to his summer studio.

Matisse was lucky that the landscape outside the open window in Collioure wasn't devastated by bombs. The town hadn't been invaded by a foreign military. Life continued in the tiny fishing village as it had before. Except to Matisse, it didn't look the same.

Why is this important? Because our changing perspective can affect our observations. If we interviewed Matisse and asked him what color the sea was in 1914, and he said "black," it would not be a lie. The sea might appear blue to us but truly black to him.

Our perspective can change because of many different things. How a person feels about something today, how they describe something today, may be very different from how they will feel about it or describe it in the future. When gathering information, keep this in mind since perspective can add to a story or take away from it. You might even revisit the same scene and see if a new perspective offers different information.

Now that we've learned how to gather information, even what's hidden or upside down, we need to figure out which pieces are the most important. To do that, we're going to take a page from one of the most elite intelligence organizations in the world: the Central Intelligence Agency (CIA).

CHAPTER 6

TRAIN LIKE A SPY ON WHAT'S MISSING

WHETHER IT'S FILLING IN THE BLANKS OR SETTING OUR feet in motion at the sound of a predator, we've learned how our wonderful and powerful brains will kick into action for our benefit even before we know it. Keeping this in mind, though, we have to stay one step ahead when it comes to thinking about what we've seen, or our brains will take over.

We can't physically or mentally follow up, hunt down, or investigate every single piece of information we uncover—at least not all at once. If we don't actively decide which task to deal with first, our brains will choose for us based on our built-in perceptions and biases. What we label In our minds as the most or least important determines what we *act* upon.

We can successfully sort through all the available information and bring the most important facts to the top by doing what the CIA does, asking three easy questions:[73]

    1. What do I know?

    2. What don't I know?

    3. What do I need to know?

WHAT DO I KNOW?

Great news! You've been doing this the entire book: collecting the who, what, where, and when.

Let's practice one more time with the following painting:

Use all the observation techniques we've learned so far, and list all the facts you can find. I'll start: there is a train coming out of a fireplace.

Now check off if you wrote the following:

- ☑ Smoke or steam is puffing from the engine's smokestack.
- ☒ The fireplace has a grayish-white pattern.
- ☑ There is a clock on top of the fireplace.
- ☑ There is a mirror on top of the fireplace.
- ☒ There are two candlesticks on top of the fireplace.
- ☑ The clock is black with a round white face.
- ☑ The clock has Roman numerals on it.
- ☑ The mirror has a gold frame around it.
- ☑ The candlesticks are brown or bronze colored.
- ☑ The candlesticks have "bumps" or "knobs" on them.
- ☑ The floor is made up of wood planks.

What about the smaller details? Did you note any of the following?

- ☒ There are fifteen wooden planks on the floor.
- ☑ The locomotive has ten wheels, only six of which we can see.
- ☑ There's a red bumper on the front of the train.
- ☒ The time on the clock is about 12:42.
- ☑ The shadow of the train in the fireplace is pointing in a southwest direction.
- ☑ Only the left candlestick is reflected in the mirror.
- ☑ The steam from the train flows up into the chimney instead of out into the room.

 The actual word for the bumps on a candlestick? Knops

111

Now let's decide which facts from both sections are the most important. Copy the table below onto a separate sheet of paper.

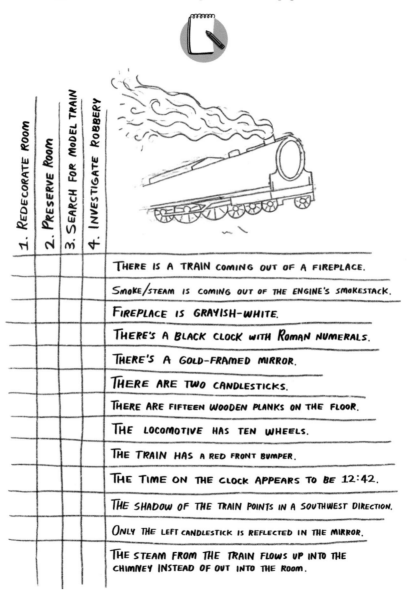

1. Redecorate Room	2. Preserve Room	3. Search for Model Train	4. Investigate Robbery	
				There is a train coming out of a fireplace.
				Smoke/steam is coming out of the engine's smokestack.
				Fireplace is grayish-white.
				There's a black clock with Roman numerals.
				There's a gold-framed mirror.
				There are two candlesticks.
				There are fifteen wooden planks on the floor.
				The locomotive has ten wheels.
				The train has a red front bumper.
				The time on the clock appears to be 12:42.
				The shadow of the train points in a southwest direction.
				Only the left candlestick is reflected in the mirror.
				The steam from the train flows up into the chimney instead of out into the room.

Let's examine how the level of importance changes for each situation depending upon who is analyzing it.

Pretend you are an interior designer called in to completely redecorate this room. On your table, in Column #1, mark the facts that might be the most important to you.

Imagine you are a member of the town's historical society in charge of preserving this room. What would be the most important now? Mark them in Column #2.

What if you were a model train collector looking for the most unique engines in the world? In Column #3, mark the facts important for this scenario.

Suppose you are a detective investigating the scene of a robbery. How would the order of importance change? In Column #4, mark each fact you believe now to be the most important.

We can see how what's most important changes depending on the circumstances and who's looking. For a model train enthusiast, the most important things in the room would have to do with the engine. For a police officer investigating a robbery, it would be the time on the clock.

Even when the order of importance remains the same, the reasons for those priorities are different. Both an interior designer and a historical preservationist would be most concerned about the wood floor and existing fireplace. However, a designer might be looking at these two items to change them to the new homeowner's liking, while a historian would want to make sure they were saved. There is no right or wrong way to prioritize; it just depends upon each person and each situation.

Let's look at another example of how the same situation can be prioritized differently by different people.

Say that an elevator in an apartment building screeches to a halt and stops working.

The following people are involved:

1. A repair person
2. The building's owner
3. A tenant on floor five whose laundry needs to be washed in the basement
4. A young college student on floor three who is on their way to meet friends
5. People stuck inside the elevator

Here are some of the issues regarding the elevator getting fixed:

- Which replacement parts are the safest
- How much the repair will cost
- How long the repair will take

Which person(s) will be most concerned about how much the repair will cost?

Probably #2, but also maybe #4. The building owner will care because he has to pay for it. The young college student might also worry about the price because if the owner decides to raise the rent to pay for the repair, it might affect the student's budget.

Which person(s) will find the safety of the replacement parts most important?

Definitely #1, but hopefully also #2. The repair

person's reputation, and possibly even his physical well-being, is on the line if he doesn't get the best parts to make the repair. The building owner should also want the best equipment, especially if he ever rides on his own elevator!

Which person(s) would want the time it takes to fix the elevator to be the number one priority?

Unless they are happy to be avoiding work or homework, #5 should be screaming that nothing is more important than getting them out as fast as possible. Number 3 might also think this is the top priority, but most likely wouldn't rank it quite as high as #5, since there are alternatives to her getting to her clothes, like taking the stairs.

Everyone involved has the same goal: to get the elevator moving again. How they prioritize which information is the most important to solve the problem, however, will change drastically based on who they are and what they need.

When you are collecting data about a situation, note the motives of people and their priorities. Just because someone believes something is the most important piece of information doesn't automatically make it true.

WHAT DON'T I KNOW?

This is very similar to the previous question except this time, instead of searching for what's there, we'll search for what isn't.

In many instances, what is not present is just as important as what is. This concept is called the pertinent negative in the medical field.[74] Not surprisingly, since author Arthur Conan Doyle was a doctor himself, Sherlock Holmes was exceptional at using the pertinent negative to uncover more information. For instance, in the short story "Silver

Blaze," Holmes is investigating a murder.[75] When a Scotland Yard inspector asks if there is anything odd to report, Holmes replies that there's "the curious incident of the dog in the night-time."

"The dog did nothing in the night-time," the inspector replies.

"*That* was the curious incident," Holmes says.

The dog's failure to bark was the clue that broke the case and pinpointed the murderer as someone the victim (and the victim's dog) knew.

The absence of an object, event, or behavior can help solve a situation. When we are observing what we see, we must also note the information we *don't* see, especially if we're expecting it to be there.

Go back and look at the train painting on page 110 and look for what's missing. Again, I'll start: there are no people in the room. Study the image and see what else you can think of that should be there but isn't.

Did you catch that the following things are missing?

- There are no candles in the candlesticks.
- There are no tracks under the train.
- There is no fire in the fireplace.

By pointing out what is missing, we are giving a more accurate and complete description of the room. If we just say, "There are candlesticks on the mantel," at least half our listeners will assume there are candles in them. Similarly, if you ask someone to draw a fireplace, chances are they'll put some logs and a fire in it. That's what fireplaces are for. So, to accurately describe the scene, we need to specifically mention the missing candles and fire because if we don't, other people, especially those who can't see the picture, will just assume they were present. This might not seem like a big deal now, but it could be the very thing that leads to a big break in understanding what's in front of us, the missing solution, or a clue we might otherwise never have gotten.

IN 2016, A TEENAGER IN MICHIGAN USED THE PERTINENT NEGATIVE TO HELP THE LESS FORTUNATE IN HER CITY. While walking through downtown Detroit for a Martin Luther King Jr. Day procession, she noticed something missing from her fellow marchers. Although the temperature on the January morning was below freezing, most of the people walking, including many children, didn't have hats and gloves. It was such a simple thing that she had always taken for granted, but, she found out, that hats and gloves were critical in protecting fingers and toes from the permanent dangers of frostbite—a deadly condition that can happen in as little as five minutes. Determined to fix the problem, she started a collection at her high school. Her charity, Warm Detroit, has since expanded to five other schools and delivered more than six thousand hats and gloves to homeless shelters in her area.[16]

Noticing the pertinent negative and talking about what we don't know can be as important as identifying what we do know.

WHAT DO I NEED TO KNOW?

The final question to ask in any situation: If I could access more information about this scene or situation, what would I want to know? This can help us figure out where we need to dedicate our time and resources.

Let's practice with the print of the Chinese warrior Hu Sanniang back on page 63. In Chapter 4 we assessed it in detail, and in the end, there were many things we did not know.

We did not know:

- What battle Hu Sanniang was in
- Her age
- Where she lived
- Why she had a horse
- The name of the horse
- Where exactly she was
- What time it was
- What she was thinking
- Who was shooting arrows at her
- Why they were shooting arrows at her
- How long she had been under attack
- What she was doing before the attack

Now imagine you were a historian. What would be most important for you to find out?

Pretend you were Hu Sanniang's mother. Are there pieces of information that would be most important for you to know different from those of the historian?

Congratulations! You've just created a personalized priority list of exactly what things you would need to work on finding out first, whether you were a historian or a worried mom.

PUTTING IT ALL TOGETHER

Let's practice prioritizing with our three-question method on the following photograph. Look at it closely for a few minutes.

What do we know? There's a two-story, yellow-painted house on fire being attended to by a fire truck with a telescoping ladder behind a pumpkin patch at McLean's Farm Market in autumn. There are pumpkins stacked in front of a stall and scattered along the ground. Some of the pumpkins are smashed. There is a person in a yellow coat looking at a pile of pumpkins.

What don't we know? Where the pumpkin patch and house are located. How the fire started. Why the customer shopping for pumpkins seems so unconcerned about the blaze in the background.

What do we need to know? Why the house is on fire and why the person doesn't seem to care about it.

Let's start with the first: Why is the house on fire? There doesn't appear to be any cause in the photograph. There isn't a cloud with lightning or a box of matches. We don't see any people except the pumpkin shopper. Let's look at them then.

The person is wearing a bulky yellow coat, which, considering the chilly temperature possible in the fall, isn't that unusual. What if I told you they are also wearing a helmut and rubber boots? Wat kind of person wears a helmut, boots, and a yellow coat? A firefighter. It is a fireman. Let's analyze this new fact.

Why of all people would a fireman be casually picking pumpkins in front of a house on fire? Could he possibly not know about it? Let's use our other senses to gather information and see.

What would the scene sound like?

There would probably be noise from the sirens or truck, the sound of the fire burning, and the roof collapsing.

What would the scene smell like?

The fire is large enough that there would most likely be the smell of smoke in the air. Based on these observations, chances are the fireman knows about the fire. And he's still looking at pumpkins.

When is a firefighter not concerned about a fire? When he knows it was set on purpose for a good reason.

Why would a fire be set on purpose? As a training exercise to help firefighters learn how to better fight fires.

Now we know why the house is on fire: to help train firefighters.

Let's impress the CIA with another three-question analysis. This time using yours, mine, and law enforcement's favorite snack: donuts.[*77]

Grab a piece of paper and answer the following questions about the photo on the next page:

1. What do I know?
2. What don't I know?
3. What do I need to know?

What do we know? There are two donuts, and what appears to be a third food item (a bagel? a scone?) in the top right, on white paper doilies on a silver metal tray under a clear dome that looks like glass or heavy plastic. The donut on the right is a medium-brown color and has what might be a very light coating of glaze. It looks dense and could be a cake donut. The donut on the left is a lighter yellow color covered with thicker, cracked white glaze. It is flatter than the other donut and appears less dense. It could be a yeast donut. Most importantly, the donut on the left IS SQUISHED UNDER THE RIM OF THE DISPLAY DOME!

What don't we know? How the donut got squished. How long our donut friend has been trapped like this. If anyone has tried to save the donut. Oh, and where the donuts are, who owns them, if they have filling inside them, how much they cost, and if they are close enough to us right now that we could drive over and rescue them. For our bellies.

 Cops became associated with donuts, not because of the actual treat but because coffee and donut shops were the only places open during the odd hours they worked, like early mornings and late nights.

What do we need to know? Why, oh why, would anyone squash a perfectly good donut like this, and why hasn't anyone else noticed and fixed it?

🍩 🍩 🍩 🍩

The situations we stumble upon aren't always as serious as a house on fire. Most of the time we're called to use our observation skills on scenes from everyday life. Take donuts, for instance.

For centuries, people around the world have enjoyed fried pastries. Gooey dough, once thrown into a hot pot of oil, would transform into a crispy-on-the-outside, soft-on-the-inside treat easily held, carried, and eaten. Different cultures flavored and decorated their creations in a variety of ways.[78] Jewish bakers stuffed their *sufganiyot* with jelly. South Africans coated their braided *koeksisters* with lemon juice. In Syria, the sticky dough balls called *awameh* were served on skewers. All the creations shared one common trait though: they were solid. Until a sixteen-year-old boy came along and changed everything.

When immigrants began moving to America in the eighteenth and nineteenth centuries, they brought their dough deliciousness with them. According to *Smithsonian* magazine, a Dutch mother, in 1858, named Elizabeth Gregory made sure her teenage son Hanson took some of her *olykoeks* ("oily cakes") when he went to work as a cabin boy on a ship off the coast of Maine.[79] She made the tastiest treats in town, thanks to a cinnamon and nutmeg flavoring, but she disliked how sometimes her *olykoeks* were undercooked in the middle. To solve the problem, she started stuffing them with nuts. Supposedly, the Gregory family called the result "doughnuts" (often shortened to "donuts") and the name stuck.

Although the dessert had been around for generations, Hanson actually didn't love it. He wasn't a fan of nuts, so he started poking out the center of his donuts. While it was a messy business, he noticed the change had some great benefits. His stomach no longer felt as heavy after he ate them since oil usually pooled inside the middle of the cakes. If the donut was punctured before frying, he found it cooked more evenly. And, perhaps best of all, a hole in the donut made it easier to carry—or store on the handles of the ship's steering wheel when a sudden storm blew in, as legend has it Hanson, who eventually became a sea captain, liked to do.[80]

Even though he was only a kid, he wasn't a trained chef, he probably didn't want to upset his mother, and fried dough cakes had been made the same way for as long as anyone could remember, Hanson Gregory persisted with his idea. He experimented with stamping out the holes using the top of a pepper shaker to make a neater circle, then asked a local tinsmith to make him a custom donut hole cutter.[81] His modification was so popular with friends and family that it soon spread around the country. A hungry boy's simple innovation changed the shape of American donuts forever.

After identifying the importance of what's there and what's not, take a few moments to think if something *should* be missing. Sometimes it's easier to focus on a problem, see a solution, or even enjoy a reward if, like Hanson, we consider what might not be needed at all.

Prioritization helps us put in order what we've already collected. Now we just need to learn how to talk effectively about what we've discovered.

How to **TALK** About What You See

"THE DIFFERENCE BETWEEN THE ALMOST RIGHT WORD & THE RIGHT WORD IS REALLY A LARGE MATTER—'TIS THE DIFFERENCE BETWEEN THE LIGHTNING-BUG & THE LIGHTNING."

—Mark Twain

How your teacher explains it	How a YouTuber explains it	How your older sibling explains it	How it actually is

CHAPTER 7

WHY MICKEY MOUSE CAN'T POINT

SEEING WHAT OTHERS MAY NOT OR NOTICING SOMETHING that could change everything is only half the battle. We can have the best observational skills in the world, but if we can't talk about what we see, it doesn't do us or anyone else any good.

It's easy to assume that everyone understands what we're saying because it's clear in our mind, but we need to make sure it's clear through our words as well.

Let's see how we stand on this skill.

1. Take a blank piece of paper and a pen to someone else. Ask them to draw what you describe. Don't look at their paper while they are drawing.

2. Set a timer for one minute. Without showing them the following photograph on page 128, describe it to them.

3. When time is up, compare their drawing to the photograph.

How similar are they?

What do you see that they are missing?

Did you mention that thing to them?

Ask them if the photograph is what they pictured in their head. Ask them what you could have said to them to make their drawing more accurate.

4. Now switch places. Have them find a picture from the next

chapter that you haven't seen yet. (If you've already flipped through the book, they can choose any other image.) Set the timer to one minute. Take the paper and pen and draw what they describe.

5. When the time is up, compare your drawing to the image they chose.

How similar are they?

Is the image what you had pictured in your head?

What could they have said to make your drawing more accurate?

It's not easy describing something to someone else, especially if they can't see it! But that's often our reality. We don't need to describe what other people can see when they're next to us. When we're communicating, it's usually about an item or an incident the other person hasn't seen or doesn't know. So, how can we make this easier?

THE COLOR OF YOUR WORDS

To create their work, artists must choose which materials to use, such as paint or stone, brushes or chisels. Even the decision of what colors to use is extremely important for artists; otherwise their paintings might be a mess or hard to decipher. In the same way, we must decide ahead of time which words we will choose when communicating to make sure we are painting the most accurate picture possible.

Think about words like colors. Some words scream, such as neon colors. Some words are soft, like light pastels.

Grab a piece of paper and write down this list of words:

Terrible

Beautiful

Lying

Best

Cheater

Wonderful

Hate

Disgusting

Unfair

Now color the words based on the way they sound.

- Color the angry words **purple**.
- Color the blaming words neon green.
- Color the encouraging words **pink**.

(*Answers: Angry/Purple words: terrible, hate, disgusting, Blaming/Neon Green words: lying, cheater, unfair, Encouraging/Pink words: beautiful, best, wonderful*)

Think about the words you regularly use. What color are they? Is that color the best choice for what you are trying to say? Are you covering your parents with a purple when a light pink might work better? Do you use neon green for your older sibling when they might listen more to a paler green?

To share the facts you have gathered about a situation, try not to use very colorful words, either positive or negative, because those words can put a filter on what you are saying and how someone hears you. If you describe lunch as "disgusting," the person who made it might not want to listen to your suggestions. "Disgusting" is a description, and it might be true for how you feel about the meal, but it's personal to you. It's also not a fact but an opinion. Someone else might think the same food was "delicious."

Grab a piece of paper and write down the following words:

Amazing

Horrible

Lovely

Three

Ugly

Paint

Great

Blue

Stupid

Fantastic

- On your list, color all the positive words bright green.
- Color all the negative words **bright red**.

The words you should have colored green are: amazing, lovely, great, fantastic.

The words you should have colored red are: horrible, ugly, stupid.

You should have some words that weren't colored: three, paint, and blue. Those are neutral words that describe facts. We call them "objective" because they describe objects, not feelings. Colorful, opinion words are called "subjective," since they describe how a subject, the speaker, feels about something.

Subjective Words	Objective Words
	three
	paint
	blue

amazing HORRIBLE STUPID lovely GREAT FANTASTIC ugly

When you want to communicate your feelings, feel free to use subjective words. But if you need to communicate facts, choose objective words. The most common objective words include numbers, colors, size, sounds, position, placement, materials, location, and time.

Let's practice. Decide if each word is subjective or objective:

1. crayon: subjective / objective
2. funny: subjective / objective
3. hidden: subjective / objective
4. gross: subjective / objective
5. easy: subjective / objective
6. noon: subjective / objective

Answers:

1. Objective. A crayon is an object.
2. Subjective. Not everyone thinks the same thing is funny, like pretending to stick crayons up your nose. I hear art teachers especially don't like that prank.

3. Objective. If the art teacher chooses to keep her crayons hidden, they'll stay hidden, no matter how much you promise not to do the nose trick again.

4. Subjective. Some people in other countries think peanut butter tastes gross, but most Americans love it.

5. Subjective. It might be easy for one kid to get peanut butter out of their braces but not easy for another.

6. Objective. Noon is a time, a fact that can't be changed . . . even if you wish you could because you got lunch detention (it was the crayons, wasn't it?) and have to eat your peanut butter sandwich at the principal's desk.

If you're not sure if a word is subjective or objective, ask another person. If the word means something different to someone else, it's probably subjective. Objective words don't change. A backpack is a backpack. Six apples are six apples no matter who is looking at them.

BE PRECISE

The more precise you are with your words, the more objective you will be. Instead of saying "small," include a measurement, estimation, or comparison. "Small" might mean different things to different people: a ladybug is small compared to a dog, but a dog is small compared to an elephant. Adding numbers will help remove doubt. "Small" is subjective; "one inch across" is not. Measure whenever you can, estimate when you can't, but try to use numbers.

If you are unable to measure something, compare it to another item. Saying something is "smelly" or "smells bad" is subjective. What smells bad to some people—like cut grass or gasoline—smells wonderful to others. Instead, find a concrete noun to compare with the smell you're describing: "The room smelled like dead fish."

Let's look at the following photograph:

Instead of saying there are "many" horses in the image, be precise. "There are eight horses." Rather than stating "there are a few trees," be precise. "There are four trees with green leaves in a row behind the horses."

Which statement below is objective, and which one is subjective?

1. Statues of horses gallop excitedly through a fountain in a marble plaza.

2. Statues of horses run through a fountain in a stone plaza.

The first sentence is subjective because it assumes that the horses are excited. Perhaps they are running because they are scared or happy.

The first sentence might seem like it has more detail—"gallop" versus "run" and "marble" versus "stone"—but these are guesses. We don't know for a fact if the horses are galloping. Maybe they're trotting. We don't know if the stone is made of marble or something else, like granite or concrete. If we state it as a fact, people who get their information from us will assume it's a fact, not knowing it's our best guess. We are misleading them without even realizing it!

BE SPECIFIC

If you go to the store and ask for "blue paint," there's no telling what you'll get. Paint can mean many things. Paint can be watercolor, oil, acrylic, or pastel. Paint can come in a can or spray from an aerosol. Paint can be thick or thin, toxic or edible, fast or slow drying. And "blue" can mean light sky blue, gray blue, neon blue, navy blue, or a hundred shades in between.

To avoid similar confusion with our descriptions, we need to be as specific as we can.

Instead of saying "car," say the type of car, such as "SUV."

Instead of saying "dog," say "German shepherd."

In the same way, we shouldn't say "mother" if we can't prove it; instead, use "woman with child." Saying "on this side" isn't specific enough, especially for someone not standing where you're standing and seeing what you see; instead, give an exact position: "to the far left."

I once showed a group a portrait, and one of the participants described the person in the painting as having "clown makeup." Which painting do you think I was showing them?

The painting I was showing them was the one on the left. The woman in the portrait did have red splotches on her cheeks and red, pursed lips, but she was not wearing the actual makeup of a clown. There was no white paint, circles, or any other indication that might suggest a circus. The description of "clown makeup" was subjective and not nearly specific enough. Another person in the same group gave a much better description: "There's a woman with a red mark on her right cheek in the shape of a baby's footprint." Perfect! Objective and precise.

Let me give you an example. California artist Christian Alderete was chosen by Pasadena to create a colorful city mural on the wall of a building. He spent more than two months on the Mayan- and Aztec-themed, sixty-foot masterpiece, and got thirty local kids to participate as well. But just a couple of months after it was completed, it disappeared. Someone painted over the entire thing.

The owner of the building decorated by Alderete's art had received a letter from the city warning them to repaint a wall or face being shut down. Which wall wasn't specified, so the owner painted the wrong one. Not being specific cost an entire California town a community work of art.[82]

Things that are specific provide more detail. For instance, look at the paintings on the next page. Both paintings that follow show a female figure in green.[83] The one to the left, however, is more specific. We see the color of her hair and skin, how tall she is relative to the dresser she's standing next to, how old she is, where she's looking, and if there is anything in her hands. We don't know any of that information in the painting on the right.

SPECIFIC

NOT
SPECIFIC

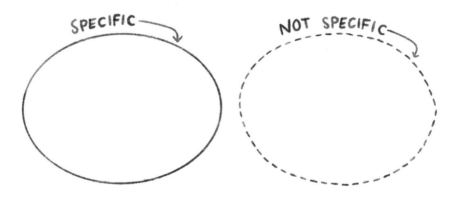

To practice choosing specific words, get a separate piece of paper and draw two large circles like so:

SPECIFIC

NOT SPECIFIC

Now, take the words from the following list and write the ones that are *specific* in the solid circle and the ones that are *not specific* in the circle with the dotted line:

Dark

Charcoal gray

Several

Six

Game

Soccer

Six-inch

Long

Heavy

Ten-pound

Student

College sophomore

Old

One hundred years

Goldfish

Pet

Flower

Rose

(*Answers: The words that should be in the left,* specific *circle are: charcoal gray, six, soccer, six-inch, ten-pound, college sophomore, one hundred years, goldfish, and rose. The words that should be in the right,* not specific *circle are: dark, several, game, long, heavy, student, old, pet, and flower.*)

BE CONCISE

Excellent communicators are also concise. They make every word count. To practice this skill, look at the following photograph and describe it in just one sentence.

Did you include any of the following words?

☑ Woman
☑ Child
☒ Black
☑ Church
☑ Pew
☒ Sitting
☑ Hand
☑ Face

If you did, good! Those are the most important. Hopefully you didn't write "mother" or "her child," as that would assume a relationship that might not be true. It might be a friend or an aunt or a neighbor.

You might have noticed other details that are true but are not as important, like circular light, boots, striped shirt, jeans, and cross-legged. Remember to prioritize.

Did you include any of these words to describe the woman?

upset

crying

sad

agitated

distressed

The little girl *does appear to be* comforting the woman. Her hand on the woman's cheek is gentle. Her face is calm, possibly worried. But the girl is young, and she might not understand what is going on.

The woman has her own hand to her face, which is twisted with emotion, but can you tell what kind? Is she upset, sad, or agitated? Is she crying? She might be, although we can't see any tears.

It's tempting to immediately see the woman on the ground, her face emotional, and think that she's upset, but that is an assumption. It might be true, but we need facts to back it up. Let's look at the rest of the photograph.

What are the other people around the woman doing?

Are they upset?

We can only see four faces, but none of those individuals appears to be upset. A woman in the back is smiling and has her hands in the air. Maybe she's clapping?

The body language of everyone besides the woman and child is also important. They are all looking forward, past the woman. No one looks at her or reaches down to help her. If someone were in distress, wouldn't the people around her react?

What is going on in the photo? There are people in a church, looking at someone or something in front of the woman. A woman is smiling and possibly clapping. A man in the aisle is also smiling and holding something pointy. If we look closely, we can see it's a microphone.

Things we do not know: Who is the woman? What is going on? Where is the church? When is this taking place? Answering these might tell us the most important information: why the woman is on the floor.

The photographer who took the photo, David Goldman, can give us some of the answers:

Who is it? The woman seated on the floor is Latrice Barnes. The child is her daughter Jasmine Redd, age five.

Where is it? The First Corinthian Baptist Church in Harlem, in New York City.

When is it? Tuesday, November 4, 2008.

Let's piece the story together now. Does that date have any significance? Yes, it does. It's the day Barack Obama was elected the first Black president of the United States.

Latrice Barnes was on the floor of the church because she was overcome with happiness at the historic election results. She might be crying, but they are tears of joy and hope, not despair or anguish.

We can't know more than we can observe, but if we had made the leap and assumed the woman was crying because she was upset, that assumption or incorrect information might have led someone else down the wrong path.

Now I want you to describe the photo in only five words. It might not seem like a lot, but you can do it!

Here's how I wrote it:

Harlem church celebrates Obama's win.

We know what's going on, with whom, where, and when in just five little words.

CHECKPOINT

We learned about the color of words and how using objective, precise, specific, and concise ones can help paint a more accurate picture of any situation, especially when we're communicating with someone else. Now let's use those skills to talk about this sculpture:

Any idea what it is? Does it remind you of anything?

It's called *Blueberry Pie à la Mode, Flying* and it was created by artists Claes Oldenburg and Coosje van Bruggen. I'm sure you can see the flying pie in there now, but the image still probably doesn't make much sense. Desserts, at least those I get, aren't usually that big, and they certainly don't fly. As we know, though, artwork doesn't have to follow any rules. It's meant to make you think, make you feel, and get you talking. I think I love the contrasting colors and shapes and it's making me feel hungry and somehow hopeful, and I'm ready to talk about it. Are you? Good!

How will we describe something as abnormal as a flying pie to someone else, especially an adult who's used to seeing things a certain way? The same way we would for a normal object: by using objective words.

Remember, our opinions and feelings are subjective. When discussing the blueberry pie in the sky, examples of subjective words might be silly, delicious, freaky, inspiring, wasteful, or genius. Objective words would include brown, fruit, hole, plastic, upside down, or pointed.

All right, then, let's start with the basics:

What colors do you see?

What shapes do you see?

I see three main colors: white, dark blue, and tan. The most common shapes I see are circles and triangles, although some of them are three-dimensional, like the sphere of ice cream and the pyramid of blueberry filling. I almost forgot the square! The pie is sitting on the top surface of a white cube.

We've got details, so now let's zoom out and analyze the whole picture. There's no *who*, so let's figure out *what*. What do you see?

Here's what I came up with:

There's a slice of blueberry pie and vanilla ice cream. The crust is stretched out like wings as if the pie were going to take off and fly.

Let's examine those sentences. Are they accurate? We know the pie filling is blueberry because of the title, but can we confirm the ice cream's flavor is vanilla? No. It's probably vanilla, as that's the most popular pie topping, but it could be any other white flavor, like coconut or white chocolate, so we can't state vanilla as a fact. Let's fix that sentence:

There's a slice of blueberry pie and white ice cream. The crust is stretched out like wings as if the pie were going to take off and fly.

Good? Grab a piece of paper, give it to an adult, and ask them to draw whatever you describe. Now read them the sentences above. Even when they're done, don't show them the photograph. Come back here with their finished sketch.

How close was their drawing to the original picture? Let's see if we can get them closer. Let's add more specific details, like shapes and positions. How about this:

On the top surface of a white cube, there is a slice of blueberry pie set up on its back crust so the dark blue filling rises up like a bumpy pyramid. The tan triangular pieces of the top and bottom crust are folded down away from the filling and frozen out like wings. There is a scoop of white ice cream that hangs on the front of the filling just like where the head of a bird would be.

Very precise but not concise. Let's see if we can cut out some of the unnecessary words:

On the top ~~surface~~ of a white cube, ~~there is~~ a slice of blueberry pie [is] set ~~up~~ on its back crust so the ~~dark~~ blue filling rises up like a ~~bumpy~~ pyramid. The tan triangular ~~pieces of the~~ top and bottom crust[s] are folded down ~~away from the filling~~ and ~~frozen~~ out like wings. ~~There is~~ A scoop of white ice cream ~~that~~ hangs on the front of the filling ~~just like~~ where the head of a bird would be.

Editing complete. We didn't take out any important identifying information like color or shape; we only removed extra words.

Go back to the same adult, read this new description to them, and ask them to kindly draw it again:

On top of a white cube, a slice of blueberry pie is set on its back crust so the blue filling rises up like a pyramid. The tan triangular top and bottom crusts are folded down and out like wings. A scoop of white ice cream hangs on the front of the filling where the head of a bird would be.

Now show your artist the original photograph and together compare which drawing was more accurate. While you're at it, give your helper a high five and yourself a pat on the back for being such a great communicator!

COMMUNICATING NONVERBALLY

We don't only communicate with words. Body language can also say a lot. Noticing what the other people were doing in the photograph with the woman on the church floor helped us to better figure out the situation.

Every country has its own way of communicating without words.[84] If you want to tell someone you loved their food in China without using words, just give a big, noisy burp! If you cut your potatoes with a knife in Germany, it's taken as a sign that the dish wasn't cooked properly. If you want to show respect to someone older than you in India, bend down and touch their feet.

Paying attention to body language can provide a lot of information. For instance, which man from the images on the next page do you think would be easier to interview for your school blog? The man on the left who looks out towards us and has his hands folded? Or the man on the right looking away with his arms crossed against his chest?

We should also be aware of our own body language because our tone, facial expression, and posture can change the way someone else receives our message. And the people around us can notice our body language, sometimes before we do.

We should not, however, let body language replace our words. A grunt is not the same as saying, "Yes, I would like more ice cream, please." A head jerk doesn't tell us which way to go.

This is why, even though he has fingers, you'll never see Mickey Mouse point. In fact, all employees at Disney are trained never to point in public because in many countries the gesture is considered rude. Perhaps even more important though, pointing isn't precise.

If a guest at a Disney park asks, "Where is the nearest bathroom?" and the employee just points into the distance, they aren't giving the guest any real guidance. It could also signal to the guest that the employee doesn't care, that they hope the guest will ask someone else a little farther down the road.

Instead, Disney employees must use specific instructions that include landmarks such as, "The nearest restrooms are about twenty feet down on the right just past the bamboo gate that marks the entrance to the Enchanted Tiki Room. If you run into the spitting camel, you've gone too far."

We should be aware of our body language, but we must still communicate. Body language is not an acceptable substitute for saying what we see.

Now that we've reviewed good communication practices in regular situations, let's explore how to do the same when things are a little crazier.

CHAPTER 8

DESCRIBING THE RAINBOW

SOME THINGS ARE MORE DIFFICULT TO DESCRIBE THAN others. How would you describe this piece of art?

It's not easy because it's kind of like a rainbow, but not. There is one section to the upper left that shows the colors of the rainbow in order from right to left—red, orange, yellow, green, blue, and purple—but the rest of the stripes are randomly colored. I 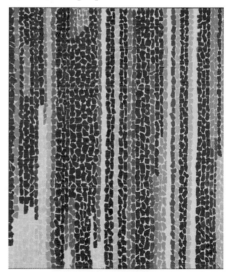 can tell you that the other colors are: gray, dark yellow, light pink, dark pink, and lavender. I can describe how each stripe is made of small blocks of color, almost as if they were ripped bits of colored paper. I'm not sure if the image is a photograph or a painting, a mixed-media collage, or a computer-generated piece, but I can say that there is no border or frame around the image.

BEAUTY IN COLOR

Can you guess the name of the rainbow artwork on the previous page?

It's called *Iris, Tulips, Jonquils, and Crocuses*, and it was painted by Alma Woodsey Thomas in 1969.[85] (The shapes are made with a paintbrush and paint.) It represents how she saw light and color reflected on the flowers outside her window.[86]

When Thomas was a little girl, she wasn't allowed to visit museums because she was Black. It didn't stop her from becoming the first person to graduate from Howard University's fine arts program in 1924. She taught junior high school for thirty-five years, and after she retired started painting full-time. In 1972, at the age of eighty, Thomas became the first Black woman to have a solo showing of her paintings at the Whitney Museum of American Art in New York City.

Since she was a Black female artist during the civil rights movement, many people expected Thomas to paint about her hard times and struggles. Instead, Thomas chose to paint beautiful and inspiring things like nature and space exploration.

"Through color, I have sought to concentrate on beauty and happiness, rather than man's inhumanity to man," she said.

Thomas reminds us that if you look for beauty in the world, you will find it, and you can create more!

When you see something that is complicated or hard to understand, you can still use objective descriptions to talk about it. You don't have to know exactly what it is or what's going on to describe it.

Take a look at this image:

Just like with the flying blueberry pie, it might be difficult to describe all at once, but if we break the image down into small, objective pieces, it will be easier.

Let's start by coming up with five specific facts about it.

1.

2.

3.

4.

5.

Here's what I wrote:

1. There is a plate on a wooden table and there is a chip on the rim toward the top of the plate.
2. We are looking at the plate from above.
3. There are thirteen star-shaped brown objects on the plate.
4. There is a cut half of a peach in the lower half of the plate toward the right side.
5. The peach does not have a pit in the center.

Let's move on to another strange image:

1. Study it for a few minutes, then write down five objective facts about it. Then cover the photograph so no one else can see it.

2. Find someone who's never seen the image. Ask them to picture the object in their mind while you read your five facts to them.

3. Now show them the photograph you were describing. Talk to them about how they pictured it based on your descriptions versus how it looks.

4. Ask them what you could have said that might have helped them to see it more clearly in their mind.

5. Give them the job of describing the photo to someone else. Then congratulate yourself for your ability to not only convey important information about unusual items but to help someone else do it as well!

Now, let's look at another curious image:

What's going on here? Who is in the image? Aside from two eyes, it's hard to tell. Maybe it's an abstract figure. Maybe it's an alien. Just because we can't use our regular *who, what, where,* and *when* questions, though, doesn't mean we can't describe it.

There's a lot going on in this painting, so list the five facts you think are most important:

1.
2.
3.
4.
5.

In real life, when trying to analyze a complicated situation, we can't just list five of the things we see. There is, however, a simple way to gather more information: ask someone else to observe with you.

MORE EYES ARE BETTER THAN TWO

Bringing in someone else, or a group of people, to help you look will greatly increase your chances of being able to find the information you need. This is especially true since every person sees and perceives the world from their own unique standpoint. Try to find someone unlike you, who isn't the same age or gender—someone with different opinions from yours.

Let's see what we gain by bringing in a fresh set of eyes. Ask a person near you to help you observe and analyze the following image:

What do the two of you see?

How many different colors are there?

List all the colors.

How many different shapes are there?

List the shapes too.

How would you describe this to someone who couldn't see it?

Was this exercise easier to do with a partner? Did they see things you missed? Especially when we're dealing with something more complex, it can be extremely helpful to share the responsibility of seeing, sizing up, sorting, and communicating information.

TOO MUCH INFORMATION

Not everything is hard to talk about because it's weird or rare or ridiculous. Sometimes it's tough because there's too much data.

For example, I'm holding a postcard of a famous painting by Claude Monet. See if you can picture it from my description:

There are no people or animals in the painting.
The scene is colored with lots of greens and yellows and blues.
It features lily pads floating on the blue water's surface.
Some of the lily pads have flowers.

Which painting do you think it is?

Are you sure? Because Monet created 250 different paintings of water lilies in his lifetime. One hangs in almost every museum in the Western world. How could you find the exact painting I was talking about based on the limited information I gave you?

People face the same type of impossible task every day. Think about an airport Lost and Found worker when someone comes in asking for their "black phone." Or a police officer trying to track down a "blue car." When there are thousands of options to choose from, the need for complete and accurate reporting is greater than ever.

So, I'll give you a hint: my Monet painting is neither of those. Here are some additional details to help you:

There are trees around the edges of the painting.

The trees are all different shades of green.

One tree is a willow that dips down into the water.

There are grassy, green plants growing on the banks.

The painting shows a bridge over the water.

The bridge appears to be made of wood and is curved upward.

In the water, you can see a reflection of the trees.

Does this painting match my description?

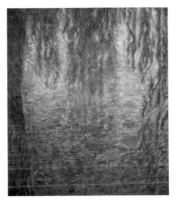

It does show lily pads on blue water. It does have a willow tree dripping into water. But what key detail is it missing? A bridge. Fantastic! So we know it's not the previous painting. All we need to do now is find Monet's water lilies painting that featured an arched bridge.

Not so fast. Monet did add the Japanese wooden footbridge that spanned a pond near his house in Giverny, France, to his water lilies paintings—eighteen of them.[87] We still need more information.

To help, I've narrowed it down to three options for you, one of which is the correct choice, I promise. Go back and read all the descriptions again, and select the one you think best matches all the data:

Alas, they all do. They all have arched footbridges in front of trees that are reflected in the water. I did forget to mention one detail, though. The Monet painting on my postcard has a shadow to the right and on top of it. Can you find my painting now?

It's the one on the top right.

Did you see the shadow? If you missed it, go back and look.

When I did this exercise with a group of military intelligence officers, one guy was devastated that he'd missed the shadow. He slumped in his seat, put his hand to his head, and kept muttering, "Oh man, I can't believe I missed the shadow!" A shadow is not a big deal to most of us, but in his line of work, missing a shadow could mean the difference between a successful mission and a failed one.

When we're describing an event or a situation we are involved in, we should look at everything, not just what's right in front of us. We should look outside the box, like seeing the shadow outside the painting, but also in the corners and off the page. Sometimes that's where the answers lie.

UNUSUAL THINGS

We've learned how to communicate more effectively in everyday, over-whelming, and even uncommon situations. But what about when we're faced with *really* unusual things? Not just flying fruit pies or wooden tables that still have their trees attached, but contradictory things that turn our brain to spaghetti? And what about when we see things that we wish we didn't? Things that scare, upset, or make us uncomfortable? We have to march ahead.

We need to talk about what we see because it exists. Ignoring it won't make it go away. In fact, like a spark that becomes a forest fire, it could grow and get worse.

In January 2021, a group of friends was snowshoeing on a hiking trail in southwestern Switzerland.[88] The day was bright, sunny, and peaceful, but it was interrupted by dogs barking. Dogs bark all the time, so the hikers didn't think anything of it, but the dogs' barks got louder. Snowshoeing is hard work, especially if you walk off the trail, but they decided to investigate anyway. They wanted to find the distressed animals to make sure everything was okay. It wasn't. On the ground in front of the dogs, a human hand was sticking out of the snow.

Two people had been buried by a recent avalanche that the adventurers hadn't seen or heard. The group dug the pair out and called for help.

The dogs belonged to the people who had been swept away by the avalanche. Their loyal pets stood watch over the spot where they had disappeared, barking to raise an alarm. What would have happened, though, if the hikers passing by had ignored the dogs' barks or not noticed the hand in the snow? The couple might never have been rescued.

But just because we shouldn't ignore what exists doesn't mean we have to pretend we don't feel a certain way about it.

Take a look at this painting:

What's your first reaction to it?

Do you like it?

Why or why not?

As humans, we all have emotional reactions to things. How can we keep our strong opinions from getting in the way of our objectivity? By noticing and acknowledging them, so we can let them go.

Describing a complex work of art with many moving parts involves looking first. The same is true when you face a difficult situation in life. Before you communicate anything, give yourself a few moments to work through your emotions so that afterward you can concentrate on seeing things as objectively as possible.

I once asked someone to observe and analyze a painting from the seventeenth century, *The Overturned Bouquet* by Abraham Mignon. They couldn't. Even though the painting was overflowing with colors and shapes and data, they just stared at me blankly.

It was the cat. They couldn't get past this image.

"It's fine if you don't like it," I said. "Just be able to tell me why."

"It looks nothing like a cat," they said. "It has these weird bat-fox ears, it's screaming like a vampire monkey, its eyes are too big and too close together, and don't even get me started on the nose! How did someone who painted such realistic flowers get the cat so wrong?"

To answer their question—because honestly, I had the same one when I first saw this painting—I showed the observer a photo of an Oriental shorthair cat. Have you ever seen one? In my opinion, they are marvelously weird-looking. As for facts: they have large, batlike ears,

big, humanlike noses, and pointy teeth like vampires! Maybe the artist didn't mess up its depiction of the cat but was painting that particular breed of cat? I suggested this to the person looking at the painting with me. They agreed . . . and seemed relieved.

Being able to talk about the subjective details that were bothering them got the issue out of the way and allowed them to concentrate on the objective details.

Let's look back at the faceless human painting on page 160. We already wrote down what we *think* about it. Now let's write about what we *see*. Remember "ugly," "creepy," and "my nightmare" are not objective descriptions.

List all the specific facts you can find about the painting.

Now describe the image in one sentence.

By flushing out the feelings, jokes, and wacky stuff you were thinking about the backward head, wrong color hair, old-fashioned scary girl out of your brain first, you were probably able to write a much more objective and useful description of the image. Bravo! Your practice is nearing perfection.

MASTERING OUR SKILLS

To prove just how far you've come, let's gather all the lessons we've learned about observation and communication and give that funky old cat-and-flower painting the works.

The Observation Period
Set a timer for three minutes and really study the image.

The Purge
Do you like the cat's face? Why or why not?

List every opinion you have about the four-legged creature.

Now take a deep breath, make like Elsa, and let it go!

The Analysis

1. Who is the subject of the painting?
2. What is happening?
3. Why did it happen?
4. What is in the vase?
5. What is on the vase?
6. Do you see the butterfly? How would you tell someone else how to find it?
7. Do you see the mouse?
8. Do you see any other critters?
9. Do you see the water?
10. What are some of the most important facts in this image?

Answers:

1. A brown, striped cat with yellow eyes.
2. A vase of flowers is tipping over.
3. The cat might have tipped it over as it was grabbing a mousetrap.

4. More than a dozen flowers, including many buds and twenty-two in full bloom. There is a variety of flowers. I could look them all up, but the ones I recognize right away include a purple iris, red-and-white-striped tulips, pink and white peonies, an orange gerbera daisy, and a branch from a flowering tree, possibly a cherry blossom.

5. The vase appears to be metal and is etched with designs, including two angels.

6. Yes. The butterfly is hovering above the blossoming tree branch on the left side of the painting, about halfway down from the top.

7. No, we can't see a mouse, but we can see its shadow in the wooden mousetrap in the bottom-left corner.

8. Yes, there are two on the walls, perhaps a snail and a spider. There are other bugs hiding in the painting, although they are hard to see unless we're standing in front of the three-foot original.

9. Of course I do! It's pouring out of the top of the vase on the right side and spilling onto the stone surface beneath.

10. That a cat is holding a mousetrap while a vase is tipping over spilling water.

Look at how far you have come! And how much easier it was to objectively analyze art compared to when you started with the first painting in this book! You have sharpened your observation skills and established a new pattern of thinking. When we choose to see the world differently with a critical eye, we are choosing to be exceptional.

THE POWER OF ACTION

When NASA and US Air Force engineer Lonnie Johnson was working on a design for a jet pump in his home workshop, he accidentally shot a stream of water all the way across the room. He instantly saw something no one else had seen before.

"I thought to myself," Johnson recalls, "'This would make a great water gun.'"[89]

He made a prototype with a large bottle of water that would release a blast from hand-pumped air pressure and took it to an office picnic.

"This major looks at me and says 'What is that thing?'" Johnson says. "I say: 'My water gun.' He then asks me if it works. So, I shot him right between the eyes. He was [furious], and totally wet."[90]

The party quickly turned into an all-out water war. Johnson's home-made water gun, which would become the Super Soaker, was a hit. He licensed it to Hasbro and has made more than $73 million in royalties from it.

Derreck Kayongo also found success in an unusual place, but by seeing something everyone else had already seen: a small bar of hotel soap.

On a business trip, the Kenyan native noticed that hotel housekeeping replaced the bar of soap in his shower. A recent college graduate on a tight budget, he went to the front desk to make sure he wouldn't be charged for the new soap.

"I already got one yesterday when I arrived," Kayongo explained. "Where is that one?"[91]

"We replace the soap every day for every guest," the concierge assured him. "No charge."

Kayongo was shocked. Every room, every day? In every hotel? Throughout America?

"What do you do with the old bars?" Kayongo asked.

"Housekeeping throws them away." The concierge shrugged.

Kayongo realized that hundreds of millions of bars were just being dumped into landfills, while many people in Africa couldn't afford even a sliver of soap. He couldn't get it out of his head.

He began driving around and collecting the used bars of soap from hotels before they were thrown away and found a recycling facility to scrape, melt, and disinfect the bars. Soon the charity Global Soap Project was born.[92] It has since recycled one hundred tons of soap and distributed life-saving bars to people in thirty-two countries on four continents.

When we recognize and act upon even the smallest of things, we have the power to change our own lives and the lives of others.

BECOMING THE RAINBOW

I want to leave you with one final instruction: never stop engaging with the world around you. It's so easy to fall into our own little cocoon, to get wrapped up in our immediate problems or personal challenges. Even though art asks us to focus on small details to understand more, don't forget to step back and look up to appreciate the big picture.

I was reminded of this on a recent visit to the Chrysler Museum of Art in Norfolk, Virginia. Hanging from the ceiling of the lobby was a massive sculpture by one of my favorite artists, Sam Gilliam. It can be seen from any floor of the

museum, but in my opinion, the best vantage point is directly underneath it. You could, of course, walk right by without stopping to really observe it. But if you stand still and look up, you are engulfed by a sea of color. The vivid stripes on the fabric installed in swooping arcs made me wonder if this is what rainbows look like from the ocean floor.

Like most people on the planet, I adore rainbows. Even though I know the scientific reason for their existence,* they always seem kind of magical, bursting forth when you least expect it, making you smile every single time.[93]

I feel the same about our wonderful, wonder-filled brains. A neuroscientist could probably do a better job of explaining how the brain works, but I can tell you how it feels: like magic. When concepts come together, when I learn a new skill, when something hidden is revealed, I am certain rainbows of color explode in my skull.

In fact, when the folks at the Human Connectome Project at Harvard University scanned a human brain using the most advanced medical imaging technology available, the pathways that carry our mental functions came out looking like this:[94]

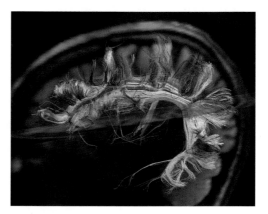

Amazing, right? Think of how much brighter your own brain is

 Sunlight holds seven different colors but looks white when they're all together. When that light hits a raindrop, going from air to water slows it down, causing each color wave to separate and bend into the arc we call a rainbow.

now that you've been using it in extraordinary ways, establishing new patterns of thinking.

You should be extremely proud of yourself. You've opened your eyes and your mind.

You've learned how to **SEE**—well, observe really, which is so much better—past internal filters, inborn preferences, and distractions. You've learned to look for the small details, the subtle changes, and what's hiding in plain sight.

You've learned to **THINK** about what you see, how to filter fact from fiction and how not to jump to conclusions or assumptions like a star basketball player. You can now gather data like the FBI, prioritize it like the CIA, and not point like Mickey Mouse. You've studied the importance of perspective, of seeing things from another point of view.

You've learned to **TALK** about what you see, with objective, accurate, precise, and concise language; even about the tough stuff, the weird, the wacky, the wrong. You've learned to question why it's always been one way and suggest a new one.

And in doing so, you've uncovered a secret world that's been right in front of you all along. You've become a super sleuth, a case cracker, a problem solver, a history maker, an editor, innovator, and advocate—all wrapped up in a bright (rain)bow. I, for one, cannot wait to hear about how you change your own life and the lives of those around you by using the fantastic abilities you were born with.

You are so SM**ART**.

Author's Note
to Adult Readers

UNCE UPON A TIME, EXPERTS BELIEVED THAT INTELLI-gence was primarily innate, that some people were just gifted with bigger or better brains. Advancements in neuroscience over the last several decades have instead shown that our brains are wonderfully dynamic and that anyone at any age can greatly improve their cognitive function. We can not only train our brains to work smarter, harder, and faster, but we can also alter their actual structure and chemistry with our behaviors and activities—a phenomenon scientists call "neuroplasticity."

As a psychiatrist with a PhD in cellular biology, Dr. George Viamontes understood more than most parents the importance of outside stimulation for brain development. To give his own sons the best possible start, he regularly challenged them to sharpen their analytical skills outside the classroom. With spoons.

Viamontes used everyday objects to challenge his sons. A favorite game to help them engage their critical thinking skills often occurred over family dinners. Viamontes would look around the room, seize an item at random, and ask his children to think about it differently.

"List as many uses for this spoon as you can," he said one night, smiling through his thick mustache, "but they can't have anything to do with food."

"You could use a spoon to dig a hole," his younger son, Christopher, said.

"True," older brother, George Jr., agreed, "but it would be better for doing something smaller, like repairing a pitch mark on a golf course."

"You could use a spoon as a mirror," Christopher said. "But only the back side, unless you wanted to look at yourself upside down!"

"If the sun was strong enough, the spoon shiny enough, and you angled it correctly, I suppose you could use it to start a fire," George Jr. said.

The brothers quickly tallied more than one hundred different uses. Art was covered ("part of a sculpture!," "a small paint palette"), as was science ("a lever," "a conductor for electricity"), math ("as a compass to draw a perfect circle"), and even candle-making ("to hold the wax while you melt it"). Once the boys realized the spoon itself could be melted and re-formed into different things entirely, the game took on a whole new level of possibility.

Viamontes's boys grew up to be actual rocket scientists who now study quantum mechanics. It's impossible to know how much their father's early brain training helped them in their future careers, but it certainly didn't hurt. Neuroplasticity shows us that the more we practice complex problem solving, the better we get at it. Good critical thinking skills are essential for every profession, not just the sciences. And they can help us and our children be better observers, better communicators, and better humans.

Much like Dr. Viamontes helped his children expand their brain-power by constantly challenging them using everyday objects, this book can help your child learn to process the information around them in a new way. Only instead of using spoons, we're going to use another everyday object that's all around us: art.

In *Visual Intelligence*, a *New York Times* science bestseller, I taught readers how to sharpen their observation, perception, and communication skills using art. I've spent the last eighteen years teaching the same skill set to leaders around the world, including at the FBI, NYPD, and NATO and I've seen how the simple, conscious act of focusing our attention on a work of art has changed the lives of people from all walks of life: from the Silicon Valley executive and the Mount Sinai surgeon to the 911 operator, the doorman, and the preschool administrator. And now I'd like to share it with you and your child.

Whether you're a parent, a caregiver, or a teacher yourself, this book will help the child you care about assess situations, adapt to new information, and analyze what's seen, what's unseen, and what could be.

The book is self-directed and interactive, so you may read it with your child or let them fly solo; in either case, many activities ask them to seek out a partner so you'll likely be hearing from and hopefully challenged by them. Be prepared to be amazed at their quick adoption of these skills—skills that will transform them to be more analytical, thoughtful, safer, and a better judge of social, political, and even stressful situations. Anyone who works on increasing their visual intelligence will reap the rewards of seeing the world in a new light. Help your child open their eyes. They might not even realize they were closed.

ENDNOTES

CHAPTER 1: YOUR BRAIN IS MAGIC

1 *Today the company*: Unilever USA. https://www.unileverusa.com/brands/food-and-drink/popsicle.html.

2 *She became a*: Agnes Hsu, "8 Uplifting Kid-Started Charities," *Hello Wonderful*, February 22, 2018. https://www.hellowonderful.co/post/8-uplifting-kid-started-charities/.

3 *When she told*: Jake Rossen, "7 Kids Who Helped Solve Crimes," *Mental Floss*, May 5, 2017. https://www.mentalfloss.com/article/94828/7-kids-who-helped-solve-crimes.

4 *In fact, it is the brain*: The *Encyclopedia of Neuroscience* officially classifies the retina as "a true part of the brain displaced into the eye during development," *Encyclopedia of Neuroscience*, ed. Larry R. Squire (Philadelphia:

Academic Press, 2009), s.v. "retina."

5 *When we engage*: Society for Neuroscience, *Brain Facts: A Primer on the Brain and Nervous System,* 7th ed. www.brainfacts.org.

6 *Scientists have discovered*: Lauran Neergaard, "At Age 40, Both Brain and Body Start to Slow," *NBC News*, Associated Press, November 3, 2008; Karlene K. Ball, Daniel L. Roenker, and John R. Bruni, "Developmental Changes in Attention and Visual Search through Adulthood," *The Development of Attention: Research and Theory,* ed. James T. Enns. (New York: North Holland, 1990): 489–492; Meghomala Das, David M. Bennett, and Gordon N. Dutton, "Visual Attention as an Important Visual Function: An Outline of Manifestations, Diagnosis and Management of Impaired Visual Attention,"

British Journal of Ophthalmology, vol. 92, no. 11 (November 2007): 1556–60.

7 *Researchers have found*: Marian Cleeves Diamond, "The Brain . . . Use It or Lose It," *Mindshift Connection,* vol. 1, no. 1, reprinted in Johns Hopkins School of Education website. http://education.jhu. edu/PD/newhorizons/Neurosciences/ articles/The%20Brain...Use%20it%20 or%20Lose%20It/.

8 *Harvard psychologists discovered*: Melinda Beck, "Anxiety Can Bring Out the Best," *Wall Street Journal,* June 18, 2012.

9 *"We are all"*: Alexander Graham Bell, "Discovery and Invention," *National Geographic,* vol. 25 (June 1914): 650.

10 *Sir Isaac Newton*: Newton, Isaac, *The PRINCIPIA: Mathematical Principles of Natural Philosophy* (New York: Snowball Publishing, 2010).

CHAPTER 2: SEEING LIKE SHERLOCK HOLMES

11 *When Doyle first*: "Arthur Conan Doyle: Physician," the Conan Doyle Estate. https://arthurconandoyle.co.uk/ physician.

12 *Doyle turned to*: Harold Emery Jones, "The Original of Sherlock Holmes," *Conan Doyle's Best Books in Three Volumes: A Study in Scarlet and Other Stories; The Sign of the Four and Other Stories; The White Company and Beyond the City* (New York: P. F. Collier & Son): 1904; Katherine Ramsland, PhD, "Observe Carefully, Deduce Shrewdly: Dr. Joseph Bell," *Forensic Examiner,* Aug 18, 2009.

13 *Due to his clear*: Carolyn Wells, *The Technique of the Mystery Story* (Springfield, MA: Home Correspondence School, 1913).

14 *Dr. Bell could*: Joseph V. Klauder, "Sherlock Holmes as a Dermatologist, with Remarks on the Life of Dr. Joseph Bell and the Sherlockian Method of Teaching," *AMA Archives of Dermatology and Syphilology,* vol. 68, no. 4 (October 1953): 368–77.

15 *"Glance at a man"*: Harold Emery Jones, "The Original of Sherlock Holmes," *Conan Doyle's Best Books in Three Volumes: A Study in Scarlet and Other Stories; The Sign of the Four and Other Stories; The White Company and*

Beyond the City (New York: P. F. Collier & Son): 1904.

16 *He was fond*: "Fiction Imitates Real Life in Case of True Inspiration," *Irish Examiner,* November 4, 2011.

17 *He concluded*: Carolyn Wells, *The Technique of the Mystery Story* (Springfield, MA: Home Correspondence School, 1913).

18 *Sir Arthur Conan:* Sir Arthur Conan Doyle, *The Adventures of Sherlock Holmes* (Vancouver: Engage Books, 2010).

19 *Radiologists are doctors*: "Test and Treatment Topics," *Radiological Society of North America, Inc. (RSNA),* RadiologyInfo.org

20 *The radiologists looked*: Alix Spiegel, "Why Even Radiologists Can Miss a Gorilla Hiding in Plain Sight," *Morning Edition*, NPR, February 11, 2013.

21 *It first appeared*: Daniel B. Schneider, "F.Y.I." *New York Times*, June 28, 1998.

22 *"proper seeing is"*: Henry Oakley, "Other Colleges Say—," *The Technique*, student newspaper of Georgia Institute of Technology, December 9, 1949. https://smartech.gatech.edu/bitstream/handle/1853/19396/1949-12-09_33_43.pdf.

23 *Multiple studies have*: Todd W. Thompson et al., "Expanding Attentional Capacity with Adaptive Training on Multiple Object Tracking Task," *Journal of Vision*, vol. 11, no. 11 (September 23, 2011): 292; Hoon Choie and Takeo Watanabe, "Changes Induced by Attentional Training: Capacity Increase vs. Allocation Changes," *Journal of Vision*, vol. 10, no. 7 (August 2, 2010): 1099; and Jennifer O'Brien et al., "Effects of Cognitive Training on Attention Allocation and Speed of Processing in Older Adults: An ERP study," *Journal of Vision*, vol. 11, no. 11 (September 23, 2011): 203.

24 *One of my students*: Dr. Allison West, interview with author, June 28, 2014. I am indebted to Dr. West not just for sharing her experiences with me but for working tirelessly to make sure the Art of Perception program would continue at NYU Medical School.

CHAPTER 3: FACTS VERSUS FILTERS

25 *Perception can color*: Daniel L. Schacter, Daniel T. Gilbert, and Daniel M. Wegner, *Psychology* (New York:

Worth, 2011): 125–71.

26 *One resident said*: Wbay/nns, "Wisconsin Sculpture Creating Controversy," WKRC, Local12.com, January 6, 2020; Duke Behnke, "Controversy over Appleton's Big Head Sculpture Invigorates the Wisconsin Artist Who Created It," *Appleton Post-Crescent*, December 20, 2019; Monique Lopez, FOX 11 News, "Neighbors Go Head to Head with City over 'Monstrosity' of a Sculpture," WLUK, December 21, 2019.

27 *Experimenters at the*: Vinoth K. Ranganathan et al., "From Mental Power to Muscle Power—Gaining Strength by Using the Mind," *Neuropsychologia*, vol. 42, no. 7 (June 2004): 944–56.

28 *As soon we*: John F. Kihlstrom, "The Cognitive Unconscious," *Science* vol. 237 (September 18, 1987): 1445–52.

29 *The scientific terms*: Daniel Reisberg, *Cognition*, 3rd ed. (New York: Norton, 2005): 469–71.

30 *Frequency illusion is*: Pacific Standard Staff, "There's a Name for That: The Baader-Meinhof Phenomenon," *Pacific Standard*, July 22, 2013.

31 *For instance, when*: David Dunning and Emily Balcetis, "Wishful Seeing: How Preferences Shape Visual Perception," *Current Directions in Psychological Science,* vol. 22, no. 1 (February 2013): 33–37; Derek M. Isaacowitz, "Motivated gaze: The view from the gazer," *Current Directions in Psychological Science,* 2006, 68–72.

32 *For instance, if*: Jason G. Goldman, *"Real Life Werewolves? Dog Bites and Full Moons,"Scientific American Blog Network. Scientific American, October 31, 2011.*

33 *For instance, a*: Gerald Häubl, Benedict G. C. Dellaert, and Bas Donkers, "Tunnel Vision: Local Behavioral Influences on Consumer Decisions in Product Search," *Marketing Science*, September 22, 2009.

34 *Our wishful seeing*: David Dunning and Emily Balcetis, "Wishful Seeing: How Preferences Shape Visual Perception," *Current Directions in Psychological Science,* vol. 22, no. 1 (February 2013): 33–37.

35 *People on a diet*: Guido M. van Koningsbruggen, Wolfgang Stroebe, and Henk Aarts, "Through the Eyes of Dieters: Biased Size Perception of Food

Following Tempting Food Primes," *Journal of Experimental Social Psychology*, vol. 47, no. 2 (March 2011): 293–99.

36 *In New York*: Emily Balcetis and David Dunning, "Wishful Seeing: More Desired Objects Are Seen as Closer," *Psychological Science,* December 2009; Kohske Takahashi et al., "Psychological Influences on Distance Estimation in a Virtual Reality Environment," *Frontiers in Human Neuroscience*, vol. 7 (September 18, 2013): 580.

37 *It isn't that*: Natalie Angier, "Blind to Change, Even as It Stares Us in the Face," *New York Times*, April 1, 2008; John Lloyd, John Mitchinson, and James Harkin, *1,227 Quite Interesting Facts to Blow Your Socks Off* (New York: W. W. Norton & Company, September 9, 2013).

CHAPTER 4: WINNING AT HIDE-AND-SEEK

38 *Abdul-Jabbar is an*: "Innovative Lives: Kareem Abdul-Jabbar," Lemelson Center for the Study of Invention and Innovation, October 3, 2019.

39 *Kareem was in*: Jonathan Blitzer, "Elementary," *New Yorker*, January 26, 2015;

Mike Sager, "Kareem Abdul-Jabbar on His 45-Year Obsession with Sherlock Holmes," *Esquire*, September 17, 2015.

40 *Because blue light*: SciJinks, "Why Is the Sky Blue?" National Oceanic and Atmospheric Administration, May 27, 2021.

41 *Since they're mammals*: "Do cats have belly buttons? If not, then how do their offspring get their nutrients?" *Science Line*, University of California Santa Barbara, May 8, 2003.

42 *It packs one*: Jessie Szalay, "Broccoli: Health Benefits, Risks & Nutrition Facts," *Live Science*, June 15, 2017.

43 *For humans, after:* Rose Boccio, "The Ins and Outs of Navels," *Chicago Tribune*, October 17, 2000.

44 *Only 10 percent*: Cari Nierenberg, "What Makes an Innie an Innie? And More Belly Button Mysteries," NBC News, May 16, 2011.

45 *Kickapoo Tribal Chairman*: Kaitlyn Schumacher, "Kickapoo High School Students Create Petition to Change the School's Traditions," KY3, February 4, 2021.

46 *Kickapoo High's principal*: Ibid.

47 *"Just listening to"*: Joe Hickman, "Springfield's Kickapoo High School Phasing Out Old Logo, Changing Other Traditions, but Keeping Chiefs Mascot Name," KY3, September 3, 2021.

48 *"We did learn"*: Ibid.

49 *"You can visit her"*: Mrs. John Winthrop by John Singleton Copley (American, Boston, Massachusetts 1738–1815 London), 1773, is currently on display in Gallery 748 at The Metropolitan Museum of Art in New York City. You can also view the painting online in the museum's collection at http://www.metmuseum.org/collection/the-collection-online/search/10531.

50 *It happens to*: Andrew J. Macnab and Mary Bennett, "Refrigerator Blindness: Selective Loss of Visual Acuity in Association with a Common Foraging Behaviour," *Canadian Medical Association Journal*, vol. 173, no. 12 (December 6, 2005): 1494–95.

51 *Sometimes, for no*: Steven B. Most et al., "What You See Is What You Set: Sustained Inattentional Blindness and the Capture of Awareness," *Psychological Review*, vol. 112 (Jan 2005): 217–242; Ethan A. Newby and Irvin Rock, "Inattentional Blindness as a Function of Proximity to the Focus of Attention," *Perception,* vol. 27, no. 9 (1998): 1025–40.

52 *Our eyes would*: David Owen, "The Psychology of Space," *New Yorker*, January 21, 2013.

53 *The ability to*: Arne Ohman, "Has Evolution Primed Humans to 'Beware the Beast'?" *Proceedings of the National Academy of Sciences of the United States of America*, vol. 104, no. 42 (October 16, 2007): 16396–97; Gervais Tompkin, "Survival of the Focused," GenslerOnWork, November 11, 2013.

54 *This instant organization*: Ming Meng, David A. Remus, and Frank Tong, "Filling-in of Visual Phantoms in the Human Brain," *Nature Neuroscience*, vol. 8, no. 9 (August 7, 2005): 1248–54; Melanie Moran, "The Brain Doesn't Like Visual Gaps and Fills Them In," *Exploration: Vanderbilt's Online Research Magazine*, Vanderbilt University, August 19, 2007.

55 *The fact that*: Marguerite Reardon, "Americans Text More Than They Talk," CNET, September 22, 2008; and Sherna Noah, "Texting Overtakes Talking as

Most Popular Form of Communication in UK," *Independent*, July 18, 2012.

56 *What you saw*: Frederick A.A. Kingdom, Samir Touma, and Ben J. Jennings, "Negative Afterimages Facilitate the Detection of Real Images," *Vision Research*, vol. 170 (May 2020): 25–34. https://doi.org/10.1016/j.visres.2020.03.005.

57 *The company paid*: Yoni Heisler, "Inside Apple's Secret Packaging Room," *Network World*, January 24, 2012.

58 *When Walt Disney*: Bruce Jones, "Success Is in the Details: How Disney Overmanages the Customer Experience," *Disney Institute*, January 9, 2014.

59 *It's not a*: "Virgin Atlantic Wins Top Customer Service Award," Virgin Atlantic press release, January 19, 2009; the tagline "We get all the details just right" appeared on the Virgin Atlantic company website under "Virgin experience" when accessed June 22, 2014: http://www.virgin-atlantic.com/gb/en/the-virgin-experience.html.

CHAPTER 5: THE PLAYGROUND MADE YOU SMARTER

60 *"Change the way"*: Thomas Boswell, "To Bryce Harper and Davey Johnson, 'Play Me or Trade Me' Is Just a Healthy Joke," *Washington Post*, July 7, 2013; Wayne W. Dyer, "Success Secrets," *DrWayneDyer.com*, Hay House, www.drwaynedyer.com.

61 *Instead of the*: While the picture might look like something clever you've seen on the Internet, it's actually by an Italian painter from 450 years ago, Giuseppe Arcimboldo. Arcimboldo was famous for his visual double entendres, creating portraits of people out of fruit, vegetables, books, and even other people.

62 *A quick Google*: Rebecca Dobrinski, "Permanent Residents: Kerry James Marshall in Birmingham," *Burnaway*, https://burnaway.org/magazine/kerry-james-marshall/.

63 *The image on*: "Chris Ofili, Blossom, 1997," *Victoria Miro*, https://www.victoria-miro.com/artists/6-chris-ofili/works/artworks703/.

64 *The Disney-ish princess*: "Kerry James Marshall at Secession," *Contemporary Art Daily*, November 20, 2012.

65 *During construction, thousands*: Thomas Smith, "Hong Kong Disneyland Unveils First of Its Kind Castle of

Magical Dreams," *Disney Parks Blog*, The Walt Disney Company, November 20, 2020.

66 *In the same*: Professor Yianis A. Pikoulas, "Cart-wheel Road Communication," *Kathimerini*, January 4, 1998; Martijn P. van den Heuvel, et al., "Efficiency of Functional Brain Networks and Intellectual Performance," *Journal of Neuroscience,* vol. 29, no. 23 (June 10, 200): 7619–24.

67 *"The very act"*: Roderick Gilkey and Clint Kilts, "Cognitive Fitness," *Harvard Business Review*, November 2007.

68 *As you do*: Drew Boyd, "Fixedness: A Barrier to Creative Output," *Psychology Today*, June 26, 2013.

69 *Henri Rousseau never*: Zuzanna Stanska, "The Fantastic Jungles of Henri Rousseau," *Daily Art Magazine*, March 14, 2020.

70 *In* To Kill: Harper Lee, *To Kill a Mockingbird* (New York: Grand Central Publishing, 1960): 33.

71 *Matisse spent countless*: Hilary Spurling, Matisse the Master: A Life of Henri Matisse, the Conquest of Colour, 1909–1954. (New York: Alfred A. Knopf, 2005): 161–63.

72 *In fact, according*: "Great Figures of Modern Art: Henri Matisse," Centre Pompidou, Paris, http://mediation.centre-pompidou.fr.

CHAPTER 6: TRAIN LIKE A SPY ON WHAT'S MISSING

73 *We can successfully*: Richard J. Heuer, *The Psychology of Intelligence Analysis* (Washington DC: Center for the Study of Intelligence Agency, 1999).

74 *This concept is*: "Pertinent Negative," *Medical Terminology,* Emory University Emergency Medical Services. http://www.emory.edu/EEMS/MedicalTerms.html.

75 *For instance, in*: Arthur Conan Doyle, "Silver Blaze," *The Memoirs of Sherlock Holmes* (London: Oxford University Press, 2009): 22.

76 *Her charity Warm*: For more information on Warm Detroit, to donate, or start a collection in your area, go to www.warmdetroit.org.

77 *Cops became associated*: Lauren Masur, "The Real Reason Cops Are Always Eating Donuts," *Kitchn*, August 14, 2018.

78 *Different cultures flavored*: "Top 50 Most Popular Fried Dough Food," *Taste Atlas*, January 30, 2021.

79 *According to* Smithsonian: David A. Taylor, "The History of the Doughnut," *Smithsonian*, March 1998.

80 *And, perhaps best*: David A. Taylor, "The History of the Doughnut," *Smithsonian*, March 1998.

81 *He experimented with*: "The Maine Ship Captain Who Invented the Modern Donut," New England Historical Society, April 16, 2021. https://www.newenglandhistoricalsociety.com/maine-ship-captain-invented-modern-donut/.

CHAPTER 7: WHY MICKEY MOUSE CAN'T POINT

82 *Not being specific*: Janette Williams, "Miscommunication May Have Led to Painting over $2,500 Mural at Pasadena Business," *Pasadena Star-News*, November 29, 2009.

83 *Both paintings below*: Left image: *Hon. Mrs Ernest Guinness* by Sir Francis Bernard Dicksee, 1912; right image: *Female Figure* by Kazimir Malevich, 1932.

84 *Every country has*: Brooke Nelson, "10 Rude Manners That Are Actually Polite in Other Countries," *Reader's Digest*, May 2, 2020.

CHAPTER 8: DESCRIBING THE RAINBOW

85 *It's called* Iris: Artsy Editors, "Museums Bring Pioneering Painter Alma Thomas Out of Storage for Her First Major Retrospective in over 30 Years," *Artsy*, January 21, 2016.

86 *It represents how*: Elizabeth Lynch, "Alma Woodsey Thomas: Hidden History," *National Museum of Women in the Arts*, September 21, 2020.

87 *Monet did add*: Claude Monet, "Bridge over a Pond of Water Lilies," *Collection Online*. Metropolitan Museum of Art, New York.

88 *In January 2021:* "Dogs' Barking Prompts Owners' Rescue from Swiss Avalanche, *Reuters*, January 31, 2021.

89 *"I thought to"*: Seth Porges, "7 Questions for Super Soaker Inventor Lonnie Johnson," *Popular Mechanics*, October 1, 2009.

90 *"This major looks"*: Seth Porges, "7 Questions for Super Soaker Inventor

Lonnie Johnson," *Popular Mechanics*, October 1, 2009.

91 *"I already got"*: Interview with author, September 2014.

92 *Soon the charity*: To find out how you can get involved, visit Global Soap Project at www.globalsoap.org.

93 *Even though I*: SciJinks, "What Causes a Rainbow?," National Oceanic and Atmospheric Administration, May 27, 2021.

94 *In fact, when*: Kat McGowan, "New Project Maps the Wiring of the Brain," *Discover*, January 23, 2013.

95 *Inattentional blindness*: Kendra Cherry, "Inattentional Blindness in Psychology," *Very Well Mind*, May 4, 2020.

ACKNOWLEDGMENTS

My heartfelt thanks to the countless students, teachers, and museum educators who taught me to use my eyes to see the world in all its colorful brilliance. Susan Ginsburg, Krista Vitola, Mary Pantoga, and Catherine Bradshaw, thank you for bringing the canvas, brushes, and beautiful hues to so many readers. And, as always, my gratitude to Ian, for letting me see the world through his bright eyes to boost my brain in the most extraordinary ways.

—A. E. H.

To my favorite young explorers: Gavin, Hadley, Hunter, Mia, Lizzie, Henry, Will, Emma, Ryan, Cassidy, Avery, Alanna, Kylie, Iain, Caedon, Sutton, Sawyer, Savannah, Carson and Chase. I see how smART you are, and it makes my heart soar.

—H. M.

PHOTO CREDITS

for *"The Spanish Dancer,"* c. 1880–1881 Watercolor, 11 7/8 × 7 7/8 in. (30.16 × 20 cm) Dallas Museum of Art, Foundation for the Arts Collection, gift of Margaret J. and George V. Charlton in memory of Eugene McDermott 1974. Image courtesy Dallas Museum of Art

8 Giacomo Balla (1871–1958) *Boccioni's Fist—Lines of Force II,* 1916–1917/reconstructed 1956–1958/cast 1968, Brass and paint, 33 x 31 1/2 x 13 in. (83.8 x 80 x 33 cm) Gift of Joseph H. Hirshhorn, 1972 Hirshhorn Museum and Sculpture Garden, Image credit: Lee Stalworth. © 2022 Artists Rights Society (ARS), New York / SIAE, Rome

9 Claes Oldenburg, *Alphabet/Good Humor,* 1975, painted fiberglass and bronze, 142× 68 × 28 in. (360.7 × 172.7 × 71.1 cm) Crystal Bridges Museum of American Art, Bentonville, Arkansas, 2008.18.Credit: © Claes Oldenburg, courtesy Pace Gallery. Photography by Edward C.Robison III.

10 Drazen Kozjan, *Sherlock*

11 Joshua Werner, *The Mind of Sherlock Holmes*

12 Trafton Drew and Jeremy Wolf. 2013 PubMed article, *The invisible gorilla strikes again: sustained inattentional blindness in expert observers.* Trafton Drew 1, Melissa L-H Võ, Jeremy M Wolfe

13 Large Letter C in Inwood. Suzanne DeChillo/*New York Times*/Redux

14 Frederick Daniel Hardy (1827–1911) *Children Playing at Doctors*, England, Late-Nineteenth Century. © Victoria and Albert Museum, London.

15 Raja Ravi Varma, (1848–1906) *Disappointing News.* The Picture Art Collection/Alamy

16 René Magritte (1898–1967) *The Portrait.* Brussels, 1935. Oil on canvas, 28 7/8 x 19 7/8 in. (73.3 x 50.2 cm). Museum of Modern Art. Gift of Kay Sage Tanguy. Digital Image © The Museum of Modern Art/Licensed by SCALA / Art Resource, New York. © 2022 C. Herscovici / Artists Rights Society (ARS), New York

17 Renshaw Cow, Optometric Extension Program Foundation

18 Renshaw Cow with Face Outlined, Optometric Extension Program Foundation

19 Tree optical illusion, Chris Gorgio. iStockphoto

20 Paul Bobrowitz, "The Collective"

21 George Segal (1924–2000) *Woman Looking Through a Window* (1980), Commissioned by the Philadelphia Redevelopment Authority, owned by the property owner. Photo by Alec Rogers © 2014, Courtesy of Association of Public Art

22 Childe Hassam (1859–1935) *The Avenue in the Rain*, 1917 oil on canvas 42 in. x 22.25 in. Courtesy of The White House Collection/White House Historical Society. Gift of T. M. Evans, 1963

23 James Rosenquist (1933–2017) *Frosting*, 1964 Oil on canvas 66 1/8 x 66 1/8 in. (168.0 x 168.0 cm). Collection of the Stedelijk Museum, Amsterdam. © 2022 James Rosenquist Foundation / Licensed by Artists Rights Society (ARS), NY. Used by permission. All rights reserved

24 Kareem Abdul-Jabbar. Photographer: Stephen Dunn. Getty Images Sport

25 Mycroft Holmes book cover (source: Amazon)

26 Picasso, Pablo (1881–1973) © ARS, NY. *Self-Portrait*. End of 1901. Oil on canvas, 81 x 60 cm. MP4. Photo: Mathieu Rabeau. © RMN-Grand Palais / Art Resource, New York. © 2022 Estate of Pablo Picasso / Artists Rights Society (ARS), New York

27 Pablo Picasso (1881–1973) *Self-Portrait with Palette*, 1906. Philadelphia Museum of Art: A. E. Gallatin Collection, 1950, 1950-1. © 2022 Estate of Pablo Picasso / Artists Rights Society (ARS), New York

28 Utagawa Kuniyoshi, *Japanese*, (1798–1861) Hu Sanniang (Ko Sanjo Ichijosei) By Sepia Times. Getty Images

29 Utagawa Kuniyoshi (1798–1861) Bukan, a Zen Buddhist (Bukan zenji) Series Beautiful Figures of Women Linked to the Sixteen Taoist Immortals (Enshi jūroku josen), about 1847–48, vertical Ōban. By Molteni Motta. Getty Images

30 Michelangelo Buonarroti (1475–1564) *David*. 1501–1504. Detail of bust. Marble. Post-restoration. Photo Credit: Scala/Ministero per i Beni e le Attività culturali / Art Resource, New York

31 John Singleton Copley (1738–1815) *Mrs. John Winthrop*. 1773. Oil on canvas, 35 1/2 x 28 3/4 in. (90.2 x 73 cm). Morris

K. Jesup Fund, 1931 (31.109). Image copyright © The Metropolitan Museum of Art. Image source: Art Resource, NY

32 "Stonebeach" Johannes Stoetter/ johannesstoetterart.com

33 Dog care photo created by wirestock: http://www.freepik.com

34 Kerry James Marshall, *School of Beauty, School of Culture*, 2012 acrylic on canvas 108 x 158 in. : © Kerry James Marshall. Courtesy of the artist and Jack Shainman Gallery, New York

35 Giuseppe Arcimboldo (1526–1593) *The Vegetable Gardener* (reversible - can be viewed upside down). 1590. Oil on panel, 35 x 24 cm. Erich Lessing / Art Resource, New York

36 Hans Holbein, the Younger (1497–1543) *Jean de Dinteville and Georges de Selve ("The Ambassadors")*, 1533. Dinteville, a French nobleman posted to London as ambassador (l.) together with his bishop friend de Selve (r.), exemplifying, respectively, the active and contemplative life. Oil on oak, 207 x 209.5 cm. Bought, 1890 (NG1314). © National Gallery, London / Art Resource, New York

37 Hans Holbein, the Younger (1497–1543) *Jean de Dinteville and Georges de Selve ("The Ambassadors")*, 1533. Detail of the skull, seen from an angle which eliminates the foreshortening. Oil on oak, 207 x 209.5 cm. Bought, 1890 (NG1314). © National Gallery, London / Art Resource, New York

38 Kerry James Marshall, *School of Beauty, School of Culture* detail, 2012 acrylic on canvas 108 x 158 in. : © Kerry James Marshall. Courtesy of the artist and Jack Shainman Gallery, New York

39 Kerry James Marshall, *School of Beauty, School of Culture* detail, 2012 acrylic on canvas 108 x 158 in. : © Kerry James Marshall. Courtesy of the artist and Jack Shainman Gallery, New York

40 Tourists visit the castle at the Hong Kong Disneyland Resort in Hong Kong, China, 12 November 2011. Imagine China Limited/Alamy

41 Henri Rosseau (1844–1910) *Exotic Landscape with Monkeys and a Parrot*, 1908. Painting Private Collection/Superstock

42 Marc Chagall (1887–1985). *Blue Circus*, 1950. Tate. © 2022 Artists Rights

Society (ARS), New York / ADAGP, Paris. Photo: Tate

43 Henri Matisse French, (1869–1954) *Open Window*, Collioure 1905, oil on canvas, overall: 55.3 x 46 cm (21 3/4 x 18 1/8 in.) framed: 71.1 x 62.2 x 5.1 cm (28 x 24 1/2 x 2 in.), Collection of Mr. and Mrs. John Hay Whitney, National Gallery of Art, Washington 1998.74.7. © 2022 Succession H. Matisse / Artists Rights Society (ARS), New York

44 Henri Matisse (1869–1954), *French Window at Collioure.* 1914. Oil on canvas, 116.5 x 89 cm. AM1983-508. Photo: Bertrand Prévost. Digital Image © CNAC/ MNAM, Dist. RMN-Grand Palais / Art Resource, NY. © 2022 Succession H. Matisse / Artists Rights Society (ARS), New York

45 René Magritte (1898–1967) ©ARS, NY *Time Transfixed (La durée poignardée)*, 1938. Oil on canvas, 57 7/8 x 38 7/8 in. (147 x 98.7 cm). Joseph Winterbotham Collection, 1970.426. The Art Institute of Chicago / Art Resource, NY. © 2022 C. Herscovici / Artists Rights Society (ARS), New York

46 McLean, Virginia, December 1978.

Credit: ©1987, 2019 for the photographs by Joel Sternfeld

47 Tara Wray, "Quechee, VT, 2014," from the book *Too Tired for Sunshine* (Yoffy Press 2018)

48 Tiger. Tierfotoagentur / Alamy

49 Kitten. Vera Shestak / Alamy

50 Pongtorn Hiranlikit / Alamy

51 Illustrated cats set. Adam Dana/ Alamy

52 A large salmon artwork overlooks the South Park Seafood Grill Restaurant, in downtown Portland, Oregon. Sculptor Keith Jellum. Larry Geddis/Alamy

53 Mustangs of Los Colinas, in Williams Square, Los Colinas, Texas. Artist Robert Glen. Superstock/Alamy

54 Vincent van Gogh: (1853–1890) *Portrait of a Woman with a Red Ribbon.* 1885. Oil on canvas. Private Collection. Painting/Alamy

55 Walt Kuhn (1880–1949), *Clown with a Black Wig.* 1930. Oil on canvas: H. 40, W. 30 inches (101.6 x 76.2 cm.). George A. Hearn Fund, 1956 (56.73). Image copyright © The Metropolitan Museum of Art. Image source: Art Resource, New York

56 Frank Dicksee (1853–1928)

Portrait of the Honorary Mrs. Ernest Guinness, Standing, Wearing an Emerald Dress and Feather, 1912 (oil on canvas) Credit: Private Collection Photo © Christie's Images/Bridgeman Images

57 Kasimir Severinovich Malevich (1878–1935) Female figure, 1928–1929 Heritage Image Partnership Ltd./ Alamy

58 Photograph at the First Corinthian Baptist Church, November 4, 2008. David Goldman/*New York Times*/Redux

59 Oldenburg/van Bruggen, Blue-berry Pie à la Mode, Flying, Scale A,1996, cast aluminum painted withpolyurethane enamel 29" x 57" x 27in. (73.7 cm x 144.8 cm x 68.6 cm) Credit: © Oldenburg/van Bruggen, courtesy Pace Gallery. Photograph by Kerry Ryan McFate, courtesy Pace Gallery

60 Paul Cézanne (1839–1906) *Man with Crossed Arms*, ca. 1899. Oil on canvas. 36 1/4 x 28 5/8 in. (92 x 72.7 cm). The Solomon R. Guggenheim Foundation / Art Resource, New York

61 Paul Cezanne (1839–1906) *Seated Peasant*. ca. 1892-96. Oil on canvas, 21 1/2 x 17 3/4 in. (54.6 x 45.1 cm). The Walter H. and Leonore Annenberg Collection, Gift of Walter H. and Leonore Annenberg, 1997, Bequest of Walter H. Annenberg, 2002 (1997.60.2). Image copyright © The Metropolitan Museum of Art. Image source: Art Resource, New York

62 Alma Woodsey Thomas (1891–1978) *Iris, Tulips, Jonquils, and Crocuses,* 1969, Acrylic on canvas overall: 60 in x 50 in x 1 1/2 in. Courtesy of the National Museum of Women in the Arts, Washington, D.C. Gift of Wallace and Wilhelmina Holladay © Estate of Alma Woodsey Thomas; Photo by Lee Stalsworth

63 Alma Woodsey Thomas (1891–1978) *Iris, Tulips, Joquils, and Crocuses* (detail), 1969, Acrylic on canvas. Courtesy of the National Museum of Women in the Arts, Washington, D.C. Gift of Wallace and Wilhelmina Holladay © Estate of Alma Woodsey Thomas; Photo by Cameron Robinson

64 Wasyl Szkodzinsky or Ron Tunison, Alma W. Thomas in her living space, 1972/73, color diapositive slide. Alma W. Thomas Papers, The Columbus Museum, Georgia

65 Still life photograph of ten-star anise and a half of a peach on a rustic stone circular plate on a wooden rustic table top. Gill Copeland / Alamy

66 Pontus Wilfors Title: *Table with Four Chairs*. Material: Wood (honey locust and white oak). Dimesions: 168" L, 146" H, 160" W. Year: 2015

67 Joan Miró (1893–1983) *Ciphers and Constellations in Love with a Woman*, 1941. Opaque watercolor with watercolor washes on ivory, rough textured wove paper, 459 x 380 mm. Signed recto, bottom center, in gouache: "Miró"; inscribed verso: "Joan Miró / Chiffres et constellations amoureux / d'une femme / Palma de Majorque / 12 VI 1941" Gift of Mrs. Gilbert W. Chapman, 1953.338. The Art Institute of Chicago / Art Resource, New York. © Successió Miró / Artists Rights Society (ARS), New York / ADAGP, Paris 2022

68 Nicholas de Lacy-Brown Composition No.1: *Squid with Patatas a lo Pobre*, gouache on paper, 2013. Copyright Nicholas de Lacy-Brown www.delacybrown.com

69 Claude Monet (1840–1926) Detail of *Water-Lilies* by Claude Monet, Musee de L'Orangerie Museum, Paris, France, Europe. Peter Barritt / Alamy

70 Claude Monet (1840–1926) Detail of Water Lily Nympheas series painted by Claude Monet at Musee de L'Orangerie Tuileries Paris France Europe. Peter Barritt/Alamy

71 Claude Monet (1840–1926) Detail of Water Lily Nympheas series painted by Claude Monet at Musee de L'Orangerie Tuileries Paris France Europe. Peter Barritt/Alamy

72 Claude Monet (1840–1926) *Water Lilies and Japanese Bridge* painted 1897–1899. Pictorial Press Ltd / Alamy

73 Claude Monet (1840–1926) *The Japanese Footbridge and the Water Lily Pool, Giverny*, oil on canvas 1899. IanDagnall Computing/Alamy

74 Claude Monet (1840–1926) *Water Lilies and Japanese Bridge*. World History Archive /Alamy

75 Ewa Juszkiewicz, *Untitled*, 50 x 40 cm, oil on canvas, 2018. © Ewa Juszkiewicz. Courtesy Gagosian

76 Abraham Mignon (1640–1679) *The Overturned Bouquet*. Oil on canvas, H 89.5cm × W 71.5cm. Courtesy of

Rijksmuseum, Amsterdam

77 Abraham Mignon (1640–1679) *The Overturned Bouquet*, cat detail. Oil on canvas, H 89.5cm × W 71.5cm. Courtesy of Rijksmuseum, Amsterdam

78 Oriental Shorthair kitten, 9 weeks old, sitting and meowing against white background. Life on white/Alamy

79 Sam Gilliam American. born 1933 *Norfolk Keels*, 1998. Acrylic on canvas, 360 x 480 in. (914.4 x 1219.2 cm)

Chrysler Museum of Art, Norfolk, Virginia. Museum purchase and gift of Oriana and Arnold McKinnon, Calvert and Harry Lester, Bridget and Al Ritter, Leah and Richard Waitzer, Helen Gifford, and Daisy Dickson 98.27 © Sam Gilliam / Artists Rights Society (ARS), New York

80 Van Wedeen, Massachusetts General Hospital, Harvard Medical School

ABOUT THE AUTHOR

Amy E. Herman is the *New York Times* bestselling author of the adult version of *Visual Intelligence: Sharpen Your Perception, Change Your Life* (Houghton Mifflin Harcourt, 2016), which has been translated into nine different languages, and the upcoming *Fixed.: How to Perfect the Fine Art of Problem Solving* (HarperWave, 2021). She is also the founder and president of The Art of Perception, Inc., a New York–based organization that trains leaders around the world to use art to improve their observation skills. To learn more about Amy Herman, you may visit her website artfulperception.com.